# YOUR APOLOGY SUCKS

ISBN 979-8-9908703-0-7 (pbk)
ISBN 979-8-9908703-1-4 (ebook)

# Dedication

MICHELLE AND I WOULD like to dedicate this book to the pain in our sides who infuriate us to no end, our beloved children: Isaac, Sammy, Leah, and Chana. You probably want us to apologize for a million things, like living further from school than you'd like, not letting you eat whatever you want, bad haircuts, pushing you guys into the pool, and not being billionaires. We know you think we're too severe on punishments and that we're unfair when we don't break your sibling's toy just to make things "fair" when you break your own.

But know that we tried and continue to try our best to give you everything. If you resent us in the future, remember that we wrote an entire book on apologies with the four of you in mind. We poured our hearts and parenting missteps into these pages (though sometimes disguised), hoping to make it a little easier for you to understand where we're coming from. Consider it our way of saying, "We're sorry" for all those little injustices you've cataloged over the years.

We love you and wish you nothing but the best in the future. We hope that all of you can embrace the healing power of apologizing in your own lives as you grow your own families. And hey, once in a while, it would be nice to hear "sorry" from you guys too, damn it.

# WE HAVE A GIFT FOR YOU

Dr. Jon Dabach has prepared a mini online video course going over some core principles from the book in detail. This mini video course is available to you for free as a special thank you for support in purchasing this book.

## GET YOUR FREE VIDEO MINI-COURSE

FREE COURSE

1. Open the camera on your phone
2. Point the camera at the QR code above
3. Open the link and enter your name and email
4. Get **free instant access** to the video course

# Contents

# 1

# Introduction

WRITING A BOOK ABOUT apologies might seem like a twisted form of masochism, but here we are. My name's Dr. Jon Dabach, and I've spent over a decade untangling the messes couples make when they bungle their apologies. Spoiler alert: it's more common than you'd think. My partner in this literary adventure is my wife, Michelle. She's a psychologist with over 15 years of experience counseling people—though she, rather wisely, avoids couples counseling like the plague. Instead, she focuses on individuals, which keeps her sane and, quite frankly, keeps our marriage intact.

While I'm the one dishing out advice in the pages that follow, Michelle's fingerprints are all over this book. She's been my editor, co-writer, and the voice of reason whispering in my ear—usually while we're decompressing in the hot tub or hiding from our four kids. Her guidance has been the golden advice that helped me better serve my patients, making sure I show up with my head on straight and my stress levels in check.

Now, why should you care about this book? Simple. Apologies are the glue that can either hold your relationship together or let it crumble into a million pieces. Most people think an apology is just saying "I'm sorry." Wrong. An apology is a finely tuned instrument, and if you play it right, it can work wonders. Play it wrong, and it's like nails on a chalkboard.

In this book, you'll learn:

- The different flavors of bad apologies—think of it as the Baskin-Robbins of relationship screw-ups.

- Why saying "I'm sorry" can sometimes feel like swallowing a live toad.

- The psychological roadblocks that make you a terrible apologizer.

- Step-by-step guides to delivering apologies that don't suck.

- How to rebuild trust and patch up your relationship post-screw-up.

We've got real-life examples that will make you laugh, cringe, and maybe even shed a tear. You'll see how mastering the art of apology has saved marriages, mended friendships, and even improved office politics. By the time you finish this book, you'll be a black belt in apologizing. Or at least you'll stop making things worse.

And hey, if you're reading this and thinking, "Man, I need help right now," you're in luck. As of this writing, I'm still seeing patients—whether it's a one-on-one session or a two-on-one showdown with your partner. If you need help with your apologies, getting your partner to apologize, or just smoothing out the rough edges of your relationship, I'd be happy to chat over the phone or a quick Zoom call. My calendar does fill up, so check in to see if there's space. Trust me, you don't want to miss this. Just go to SuckBooks.com for more information to work with either Michelle or me.

Get ready for a ride through the world of apologies. It's going to be irreverent, funny, and maybe a little uncomfortable. But if you stick with it, you'll come out the other side with a toolkit that can save your relationship. Let's get started.

# 2

# Your Apology Sucks...Why is That My Problem?

YOU MIGHT BE WONDERING why I'm writing this book. Honestly, I questioned it myself for a while. But after playing referee for couples for over a decade, I realized something crucial: the way we apologize—or, more often, fail to apologize—can make or break a relationship. If calling out your pathetic excuses for apologies (or your partner's) helps even a handful of people stop tripping over their own egos and have an easier time in their marriage, then it's worth every painful minute.

As a marriage counselor, I've had a front-row seat for over a decade on how the lack of a proper apology can erode the foundation of a marriage like termites in a wooden house. Couples who genuinely love each other end up drifting apart—not because they suddenly hate each other, but because they keep botching their communication. Apologizing might seem like a tiny act, but it's got the power to heal wounds or drive the knife in deeper.

Let me paint you a picture of a scene that happens to me at least once a week. It's a recurring theme in the soap opera that is my office: people just don't know how to apologize effectively. They fling out "I'm sorry" like it's confetti at a parade, expecting it to magically fix everything. But an apology is more than just words—it's a crucial communication tool that requires sincerity, empathy, and a genuine desire to make amends. Without those, you might as well be saying, "I'm sorry you can't handle how awesome I am."

\* \* \*

Jimmy and Chayanne arrived at my office as if stepping onto a stage, each playing their well-rehearsed roles. Jimmy, in his perpetually crisp athleisure wear, moved with the assured swagger of a man who knew his watch cost more than most people's cars. His smile, a permanent display of ceramic perfection, shone brightly, contrasting sharply with his dyed hair, a futile attempt to stave off the inevitable passage of time.

If I had the courage, maybe I'd get my teeth redone and try to pull off athleisure wear with the same confidence as Jimmy. But I'm not sure I could rock the sporty look without feeling like a middle-aged man desperately clinging to his youth. There's a certain comfort in my slightly rumpled professional attire, even if it doesn't turn heads.

Chayanne, on the other hand, wore her beauty like a carefully crafted mask. Her plastic surgeries had shaved years off her appearance, rendering her a portrait of youthful elegance. Yet, her face, frozen by the relentless applications of Botox, betrayed none of the tension that lay beneath her polished exterior. She walked with a measured grace, her movements smooth but her eyes revealing a storm of emotions that her immobilized features could not.

As they settled into the couch opposite me, the air thickened with unspoken words. Jimmy, ever the picture of nonchalance, adjusted his forty-thousand-dollar watch with a casual flick of his wrist, while Chayanne, though equally well-dressed, seemed to shrink into herself, her silence speaking volumes. The stage was set for another performance in the ongoing drama of their marriage, with hopes pinned on finding a resolution amidst the polished facades and hidden insecurities.

"So, how have things been since our last session?" I asked, diving right in.

Chayanne took a deep breath, her voice trembling but laced with anger. "It's the same thing, Dr. Jon. Jimmy's interactions with our female friends make me feel invisible. He's always so charming and attentive to them, but I feel like an afterthought."

Jimmy sighed loudly, rolling his eyes. "Here we go again," he muttered under his breath.

"Let's try to understand Chayanne's perspective," I said, addressing Jimmy. "It's not about your intentions; it's about how your actions make her feel."

Jimmy crossed his arms defensively. "Alright, but I still don't see why it's such a big deal."

Chayanne's frustration boiled over. "Imagine if the roles were reversed, Jimmy. What if I was giving all my attention to other men and made you feel like you didn't matter?"

Jimmy shrugged dismissively. "I wouldn't mind at all. It wouldn't bother me."

Chayanne's eyes widened with disbelief. "You're unbelievable, Jimmy! You just don't get it. It's not about what you think should or shouldn't bother you; it's about what actually bothers me. Can't you understand that?"

The room fell silent, the weight of her words hanging in the air. Jimmy's dismissive attitude was a barrier we had to break through. I leaned back, giving them both a moment to process. It was a small step in the ongoing drama of their marriage, but even the smallest steps could lead to meaningful change.

"Jimmy, an apology is more than just saying the words. It's about acknowledging the impact of your actions and showing a willingness to change," I explained. "Right now, Chayanne needs to feel that you understand her pain and are committed to doing something about it."

Jimmy looked at me, then back at Chayanne, his expression softening slightly but still guarded. "I don't know what else you want from me. I said I'm sorry. Isn't that enough?"

Chayanne shook her head, her voice trembling with emotion. "No, Jimmy, it's not enough. I need to see that you care, that you're willing to listen to me and understand why I feel this way. I need to believe that you love me enough to make an effort."

Jimmy leaned back, his arms crossed. "Fine, I'll try to be more aware. But I still think you're making a big deal out of nothing."

"Jimmy, imagine if every time you turned to Chayanne for support, she brushed you off or treated your concerns as trivial. How would that make you feel?"

Jimmy's gaze faltered for a moment, a flicker of something like understanding crossing his face. "I guess I'd be pretty frustrated too."

Chayanne's eyes filled with tears, a mix of relief and ongoing pain. "That's all I want, Jimmy. I want you to see things from my perspective and to care about how I feel."

The room fell silent again, the air thick with the weight of their emotions. It was a small step, but it felt like progress. Jimmy's dismissive apologies were a barrier, but there was a glimmer of hope that, with time and effort, they could find a way to truly understand and support each other.

Chayanne's patience, already frayed, finally snapped. She sprang from the couch, her voice rising in a crescendo of pent-up frustration. "You still don't get it, Jimmy! This isn't about making a big deal out of nothing. This is about our marriage, about how you make me feel like I'm nothing when you're fawning over other women!"

Jimmy, taken aback by her sudden outburst, opened his mouth to respond, but Chayanne didn't give him the chance. "You think a half-hearted 'sorry' is enough? Do you even hear yourself? You're so wrapped up in your own world that you can't see how much you're hurting me!"

Jimmy stood up, his own temper flaring. "And what about you, Chayanne? You act like I'm the worst husband in the world just because I talk to other people! You don't trust me at all!"

Chayanne's voice cracked with emotion. "It's not about trust, Jimmy. It's about respect. It's about feeling like I matter to you. Every time you dismiss my feelings, you're telling me I don't."

Jimmy threw up his hands in exasperation. "Jesus, enough Chayanne! Enough! I'm sorry, okay?! I'm sorry. I'm sorry. I'm sorry. Is that what you want?

You want me to say it a million times? I'm sorry, I'm sorry, I'm sorry, I'm sorry, I'm sorry...."

As Jimmy repeated it again and again, Chayanne's patience snapped. She reached down, pulled off her designer shoe, and hurled it at Jimmy's head. It spun through the air like a ninja star and his reflexes kicked in just in the nick of time. The pointed heel missed his face by a matter of a couple of centimeters. Without his fast moves, his eye could have been gone.

The shoe bonked off my wall and landed on the floor with a thud. Jimmy, proud of himself, looked at Chayanne with a cocky grin. "Boxing lessons are paying off, huh, baby."

She sunk back into the couch and sobbed. Jimmy looked at me, waiting for a smile or a chuckle at his joke but I didn't offer any validation. "Say whatever you guys want, that was funny," Jimmy uttered as Chayanne fought her own tears.

I nodded over to the tissue box sitting on my desk and gestured to Jimmy that he should bring them over to his wife. He sighed and reluctantly brought them over to her in silence as a peace offering.

She took the box without making eye contact and wiped away her tears. Jimmy took a deep breath, realizing how bad things had gotten, and sunk back into the opposite side of the couch. After a moment of letting things pass, I grabbed Chayanne's shoe and handed it to her before speaking.

"I know it's not in the patient intake form you guys filled out, but there is an unwritten rule that we don't throw shoes during the session. That can't happen again, okay?"

Chayanne nodded as she took her shoe and slipped it back onto her foot.

As I returned to my seat, I let the moment sit, allowing the weight of what just happened to settle in the room. The silence stretched on until Jimmy finally uttered, "This marriage has really taught me how to hate myself."

It was a rare moment of vulnerability from Jimmy that caught Chayanne by surprise. The tension started to slowly ebb away. Finally, I spoke, my tone frank and direct.

"Well, you don't have to hate yourself, Jimmy. But one thing's for sure—your apologies suck."

***

## I'm Still in Shock

I'm constantly amazed at how spectacularly people can screw up an apology. It's not just the occasional flub; it's a universal disaster spanning all ages, backgrounds, and relationship types. Whether it's a couple in their first year of marriage or their twenty-fifth anniversary, the art of a genuine apology seems to be a challenge akin to quantum physics.

Time and again, I've watched couples who genuinely love each other stumble over the simplest two words: "I'm sorry." It's mind-blowing, really, that something so basic to human interaction can be such a colossal train wreck. Just when I think I've seen it all, someone invents a brand-new, cringe-worthy way to bungle an apology, keeping my job endlessly entertaining.

## The Irony of Apologies

The irony of apologies is that they're free and seemingly simple, yet they remain one of the most challenging aspects of communication in relationships. You'd think that saying "I'm sorry" should be as easy as breathing, but for many, it's like trying to solve a Rubik's Cube blindfolded. Why is that? Why do we find it so hard to admit when we're wrong and offer a sincere apology?

One common misconception is that an apology is a sign of weakness. People act like saying sorry is admitting defeat or showing vulnerability, as if they're gladiators in an emotional coliseum. Then there are those who think that just saying "sorry" is enough, blissfully unaware that a true apology involves actually acknowledging the hurt caused and, heaven forbid, making amends. These misunderstandings make the simple act of apologizing as complicated and uncomfortable as sitting through a three-hour mime performance.

## Writing to Be Direct

In my counseling sessions, I often feel an overwhelming urge to scream at people about how epically they fail at apologizing. But, obviously, I can't do that. My role is to guide and support, not to verbally smack down or hurt feelings. This book, however, is my playground for brutal honesty. Here, I don't have to sugarcoat anything or protect anyone's delicate emotions.

The point of this book is to lay it all out there, plain and simple. I want to teach you how to apologize effectively because it's a crucial skill that can save your marriage. Through these pages, I'm giving you the tools and understanding to master the art of apology. This is my chance to be blunt, and I hope my candor helps transform your relationship.

## Learning to Fake a Good Apology

I think that even if you aren't emotionally prepared to do the work of feeling the remorse, empathy and transformation needed to offer a real apology you should still learn to fake the damn thing. You might be wondering, "Why should I bother learning to fake an apology?" Well, let's face it, even a phony, well-executed apology can stop countless stupid fights in your marriage. Sometimes, just pretending to care can be enough to calm the storm. A perfectly timed "I'm sorry" can turn a potential blowout into a minor hiccup.

By rehearsing the steps of a proper apology, you start to grasp the mechanics of what makes it effective. Eventually, these robotic motions become habits, and—shockingly—the sincerity follows. Yes, with enough practice, this always happens.

It's not about being a faker; it's about mastering the art of apology and repeating it until it's as natural as breathing. As you do this, you'll see the miraculous effects on your relationship. Your partner will feel heard and validated, which can foster that mythical deeper emotional connection and pave the way for genuine healing and understanding.

## The Transformative Power of Apologies

Consistently faking apologies can lead to a shocking epiphany: the importance of putting your partner's needs ahead of your own. Initially, it might feel like a soul-sucking chore, something you do just to keep the peace. But as you keep at it, you'll start to see the perks. Your partner becomes more responsive, arguments drop off, and the home atmosphere becomes annoyingly harmonious.

This process can spark personal transformation, even if it starts with all the enthusiasm of a root canal. When you habitually consider your partner's feelings and needs, you begin to cultivate empathy and compassion. These mind-blowing qualities are the bedrock of a strong, loving relationship. You might discover that what started as a mechanical charade of fake apologies evolves into genuine acts of care and consideration. This shift can transform not just your relationship but also your personal growth, helping you become a more understanding and compassionate partner.

## If You're Reading This for Your Partner

I get it—some of you are here because your spouse couldn't apologize their way out of a paper bag. It's a rough spot, feeling the sting of unacknowledged hurt while hoping your partner will magically develop a conscience. First off, here's a virtual hug. You're not alone in this mess, and yes, your feelings are totally legit.

Helping your partner up their apology game is no cakewalk, but it's a noble quest. It requires patience (which you've likely run out of), understanding, and a truckload of compassion. Just remember, change doesn't happen overnight, and expecting instant results is a one-way ticket to Disappointment-ville. But with the right tools and a dash of support, progress is possible. So, buckle up and get ready for the wild ride of turning your spouse into a half-decent apologizer.

**No Magic Wands, But Useful Tools**

Alright, let's get one thing straight: this book isn't some enchanted spellbook that's going to turn your partner into the perfect apologizer overnight. Spoiler alert: there's no magical fix for deeply ingrained habits. But hey, I can offer you some practical tools and mindset shifts to help tackle this issue head-on.

We'll dive into communication techniques that actually work, ways to foster empathy (because who doesn't need a bit more of that?), and strategies to encourage genuine remorse. This book won't morph your partner into the groveling, sweet-talking apologizer of your dreams, but it will give you the insights to create some positive changes.

The aim here is to arm you with the skills to navigate this tricky part of your relationship and cultivate a more understanding and harmonious dynamic. As you embark on this adventure, keep an open mind and brace yourself for a transformative ride. Mastering the art of effective apologies can deeply impact your relationship and personal growth.

Sure, this journey might be challenging—because, let's face it, nothing worth having comes easy—but the rewards of deeper connection and understanding with your partner are totally worth it. So, let's get started on this transformative journey, one apology at a time.

# 3

# The Epic Fail of Most Apologies

MOST APOLOGIES ARE TRASH. I mean, hot garbage. Picture the most pathetic, wimpy apology you've ever heard. Got it? Yeah, that's the standard we're dealing with here. Apologies are supposed to be about mending fences, right? Well, most of the time, they're about as useful as a pencil sharpener to a Montblanc pen.

So why do so many apologies suck? Because people don't actually apologize—they just go through the motions. It's like they're following a script written by someone who's never experienced human emotions. "I'm sorry you feel that way," they say, with all the sincerity of a politician promising tax cuts. Translation: "Your feelings are your problem, not mine."

Then there's the classic, "I'm sorry if you misunderstood me." Oh, so now it's my fault for not getting your divine message? Thanks, Nostradamus. Or how about the infamous, "I'm sorry, but..." Ah yes, the "but." The tiny word that transforms a half-hearted apology into a full-blown justification. "I'm sorry, but you were kind of being a jerk." Well, thanks for clearing that up, Socrates.

Now, don't get me wrong, apologies are important. They're the glue that holds relationships together. They allow for growth and perspective shifts and healing. Both my wife and I have seen amazing results for our clients in our private practice, but only if you do them right. A genuine apology can stop a fight in its tracks, rebuild trust, and even make your partner forget that in your half-awake state you missed the toilet seat and got a little bit of pee on the floor that she then stepped in (sorry again about that, honey). But to get there, you've got to drop the excuses, ditch the blame game, and, for the love of all things that are holy, stop using the word "but."

You're better than this. It's time to learn how to apologize like a grown-up. No more of this weak sauce, half-baked apology nonsense. We're diving into the good, the bad, and the ugly of saying "I'm sorry." And trust me, it's going to be a wild ride.

## Identifying Non-Apology Apologies

So, let's dive into the dumpster fire of non-apology apologies. These are the fake apologies that do nothing but throw gasoline on the flames of whatever relationship disaster you're currently navigating.

### I'm Sorry You Feel That Way

First up, we have the granddaddy of all non-apologies: "I'm sorry you feel that way." Oh, where do we even begin with this one? This gem is the ultimate cop-out. It's like saying, "Hey, your feelings are your problem, not mine. Good luck with that."

Let's break it down. When someone drops this line, they're not actually apologizing for their actions. Nope, they're just sorry that you have the audacity to be upset. It's the emotional equivalent of patting someone on the head and saying, "There, there, little buddy, your feelings are cute."

And the impact? Oh, it's a doozy. This non-apology shifts the blame right onto the recipient. Suddenly, it's not about what the apologizer did; it's about how the other person reacted. It's like flipping the script in the worst way possible. Instead of owning up to their mistake, they're subtly—or not so subtly—suggesting that you're overreacting or too sensitive. It's a masterclass in gaslighting.

Why does this suck so much? Because it lacks accountability. Real apologies are about owning your screw-ups, not passing the buck. When you say, "I'm sorry you feel that way," you're dodging responsibility faster than a politician at a scandal press conference. There's no admission of guilt, no acknowledgment of the hurt caused, and certainly no path to healing. It's a verbal shrug that leaves the wounded party feeling invalidated and even more frustrated.

So, if you're guilty of this non-apology, it's time to retire it for good. Trust me, your relationships will thank you. Because a real apology means stepping up, owning your mess, and showing that you actually give a crap about the other person's feelings. Anything less is just noise.

## I'm Sorry I Offended You

Next on our hit parade of terrible apologies is the ever-popular, "I'm sorry I offended you." Oh, the subtle art of dodging responsibility—this one's a real Picasso.

When you say, "I'm sorry I offended you," what you're really doing is pulling off a slick little maneuver. You're not apologizing for your actions; you're apologizing for the other person's reaction. It's like saying, "I'm sorry your delicate sensibilities couldn't handle my awesomeness." Not exactly a heartfelt mea culpa, right?

Let's analyze this masterpiece. The subtle shift of accountability here is a thing of beauty. You're not taking the blame for being a jerk; you're kind of, sort of, suggesting that the other person is just too easily offended. It's like offering a Band-Aid while simultaneously twisting the knife. You're taking a teeny-tiny sliver of responsibility, but mostly you're blaming them for being upset. Genius, if you're a sociopath - total garbage for the rest of us.

But here's why it's a problem: it minimizes the offender's responsibility. Instead of saying, "Hey, I messed up, and I'm genuinely sorry," you're saying, "Well, if you weren't so touchy, this wouldn't be an issue." It's a classic bait and switch, turning the focus away from your bad behavior and making it about the other person's response.

Why shouldn't this be considered a genuine apology? Because it's not one! A real apology is about taking full ownership of your actions. It's about saying, "I did something wrong, and I regret it." It's not about playing word games to make yourself look better while still kind of, sort of blaming the other person. It's a non-apology wrapped in a thin veneer of civility.

## I'm Sorry If You Misunderstood Me

Ah, the "I'm sorry if you misunderstood me" apology. The crown jewel of passive-aggressive cop-outs. This one's a double whammy: not only are you failing to take responsibility, but you're also sneakily implying that the other person is too dim to grasp your brilliance.

When you say, "I'm sorry if you misunderstood me," you're basically saying, "Hey, it's not my fault you can't comprehend simple statements." It's the ultimate backhanded apology, wrapped up in faux politeness. It's like serving a plate of insults with a side of condescension.

Let's unpack this bad boy. The hidden insult here is that you're questioning the recipient's intelligence or perceptiveness. You're not acknowledging that you might have communicated poorly or that your actions might have been hurtful. No, it's all about how the other person just didn't get it. It's a verbal sleight of hand that shifts the blame entirely onto them.

This apology fails spectacularly because it doesn't address the real issue. Instead of saying, "I'm sorry for what I did or said," you're essentially saying, "I'm sorry you're too clueless to understand my intentions." It's a masterclass in avoiding responsibility. There's no admission of fault, no genuine remorse, and absolutely zero accountability.

Why is this a problem? Because a real apology should be about owning your mistakes and making amends. "I'm sorry if you misunderstood me" is the antithesis of that. It's dismissive and invalidating. And while I've had several patients in my practice who seem to think dismissiveness and invalidation are virtues, I can assure you they are about as helpful to a relationship as leaving your dirty underwear on the floor. Instead of bridging the gap and repairing the damage, it widens the chasm by making the other person feel unheard and disrespected.

## I'm Sorry You Took It the Wrong Way

Ah, the infamous "I'm sorry you took it the wrong way" apology. This one's a real piece of work. It's like saying, "I'm sorry you're so sensitive and can't handle the truth." It's the ultimate blame-shift wrapped up in a thin veil of faux concern.

When you say, "I'm sorry you took it the wrong way," you're essentially telling the other person that their reaction is the problem, not your behavior. It's like saying, "Hey, if you weren't so fragile, we wouldn't be having this conversation." It's dismissive, condescending, and about as genuine as a three-dollar bill.

Let's dissect this beauty. The blame here is subtly—but effectively—shifted entirely onto the recipient. You're not acknowledging that what you said or did was hurtful. Instead, you're implying that the other person's perception is the issue. It's like giving someone a compliment with a slap in the face: "You look great today, for once."

This apology fails on multiple levels. First, it doesn't address the actual wrongdoing. By focusing on how the other person took your actions or words, you're avoiding any real responsibility. It's a dodge, plain and simple. You're not owning up to anything; you're just pointing out that the other person's feelings are the problem.

Why is this not a genuine apology? Because it doesn't take any accountability. A real apology is about saying, "I messed up, and I'm sorry for what I did." "I'm sorry you took it the wrong way" does none of that. It's a way to acknowledge the issue without actually admitting fault. It's like saying, "I'm sorry you got hit by the ball," instead of, "I'm sorry I threw the ball at you."

**I'm Sorry, But...**

And now, for the pièce de résistance of non-apologies: the dreaded "I'm sorry, but..." This one's the Swiss Army knife of bad apologies, versatile in its ability to completely nullify any semblance of remorse. It's like apologizing with one hand while slapping someone with the other.

When you say, "I'm sorry, but...," what you're really doing is offering an excuse disguised as an apology. It's the verbal equivalent of, "I'm sorry you're upset, but here's why you're wrong." It's a get-out-of-jail-free card for your conscience, allowing you to acknowledge the apology while simultaneously defending your actions.

Let's break down this disaster. The moment you throw in a "but," you're effectively erasing the apology that came before it. "I'm sorry I hurt your feelings, but you were being a jerk." Boom, apology canceled. It's like saying, "I'm sorry, but not really, because here's my justification." It's a classic bait-and-switch, turning what should be a moment of accountability into a justification party.

This kind of apology fails for several reasons. First, it doesn't show genuine remorse. Instead of owning up to your mistake, you're diluting the apology with excuses. It sends a message that your actions were warranted, and the other person's feelings are secondary. It's like saying, "I'm sorry, but my needs are more important than your hurt."

Why shouldn't this be considered a genuine apology? Because it isn't one! A real apology stands on its own, without qualifiers or justifications. "I'm sorry, but..." is a cop-out, a way to say you're sorry without actually admitting you did anything wrong. It's like saying, "I'm sorry, but it's your fault too." That's not an apology; it's a defense.

### Buying Your Way Out Without Apologizing

Ah, the classic move of trying to buy your way out of trouble. We've all seen it, and some of us have even tried it. But unless you have the budget of a small country, this tactic is going to get old real fast.

### The Pitfalls of Using Gifts to Avoid Genuine Apologies

So, you messed up, and instead of saying, "I'm sorry," you decide to play Santa Claus. You think, "Hey, a fancy dinner or some shiny jewelry will make this all go away." Spoiler alert: it won't. Sure, gifts are nice, and they might smooth things over temporarily, but they're no substitute for a genuine apology.

Using gifts as a band-aid for your screw-ups is like trying to fix a leaky pipe with duct tape. It might hold for a bit, but eventually, it's going to burst, and you'll be up to your knees in relationship sewage. Gifts don't address the underlying issue, and they don't show true remorse. All they do is scream, "I'm too lazy or scared to actually face what I did wrong, so here, have some stuff instead."

### Why This Tactic is Unsustainable and Insincere

Let's get real: unless you're rolling in dough and can afford to buy a new car every time you mess up, this strategy is unsustainable. Not only will it drain your wallet, but it will also drain the goodwill from your relationship. Your partner will start to see through the gifts and realize that they're just a fancy cover for your lack of genuine accountability.

And let's talk about sincerity. Nothing says "I don't really care" quite like trying to buy forgiveness. It's the relationship equivalent of a bribe. Your partner doesn't want your stuff—they want your honesty, your empathy, and your commitment to making things right. Gifts can be a nice gesture, but they should come after a sincere apology, not as a replacement for it.

### I'm Sorry, Let's Just Forget About It

Next up on our list of non-apology disasters: the ol' "I'm sorry, let's just forget about it." This one's a real classic, folks. It's like trying to hide a stain on the carpet by throwing a rug over it. Spoiler alert: it doesn't work.

### How Avoiding the Issue Fails to Address the Hurt

When you say, "I'm sorry, let's just forget about it," what you're really saying is, "I don't want to deal with this, so let's pretend it never happened." Newsflash: ignoring the problem doesn't make it go away. It just makes it fester like a bad rash. The hurt is still there, simmering under the surface, waiting to erupt at the worst possible moment.

By avoiding the issue, you're not addressing the real pain your actions caused. You're not acknowledging the hurt, and you're certainly not making amends. It's a lazy, half-hearted attempt to sweep everything under the rug, hoping it'll magically resolve itself. Spoiler alert: it won't. Problems ignored are problems multiplied.

### The Dangers of Sweeping Problems Under the Rug

Sweeping problems under the rug is like letting dishes pile up in the sink. Sure, you might avoid dealing with them for a while, but eventually, the stink will be impossible to ignore. And when it hits, it's going to be a nasty, moldy mess that takes twice as long to clean up.

When you don't address issues head-on, they don't just disappear—they grow. The unresolved hurt turns into resentment, and before you know it, you're dealing with a mountain of issues instead of a molehill. Your partner starts to feel like their feelings don't matter, and trust me, that's a one-way ticket to Relationship Doomsville.

### Using Passive Voice: "Mistakes Were Made"

Ah, the passive voice apology: "Mistakes were made." It's the ultimate way to sound like you're admitting fault while actually dodging responsibility. It's like saying, "Things happened, but let's not point fingers at who made them happen."

### Why Passive Voice Deflects Responsibility

When you use the passive voice, you're deliberately avoiding the subject of the sentence—you. Instead of saying, "I messed up," you're saying, "Mistakes were made." It's a linguistic game of hot potato, where you're desperately trying to avoid holding the blame. Passive voice is the equivalent of a linguistic fart in my opinion and should be reserved for presidential debates where obfuscation is expected.

This kind of apology is infuriatingly vague. It's like watching a magician's sleight of hand, where the blame magically disappears into thin air. By not specifying who made the mistakes, you're leaving it open to interpretation. "Was it you? Was it me? Was it someone else? I blame it on the neighbor we've never met - that guy is shady! Let's move on." Spoiler alert: your partner definitely knows, and they're not impressed.

### The Importance of Active Acknowledgment in Apologies

An effective apology requires active acknowledgment of your actions. Saying, "I made a mistake" is worlds apart from "Mistakes were made." The former is direct, honest, and takes ownership. The latter is a smoke screen that avoids taking real responsibility.

Active acknowledgment shows that you're willing to face your actions head-on. It demonstrates maturity and sincerity, and it's the first step towards rebuilding trust. When you say, "I messed up and I'm sorry," you're not just admitting fault—you're showing your partner that you respect them enough to be honest and accountable.

Own up to your actions. It might be uncomfortable, but it's the only way to truly mend the rift. Remember, a genuine apology isn't just about saying the right words—it's about showing that you're committed to making things right. And that starts with being clear about who's responsible for the screw-up. Hint: it's you.

## Being Overly Dramatic: "I'm the Worst Person Ever"

Oh, the melodramatic apology: "I'm the worst person ever." This one is a real showstopper, folks. It's like staring in your own soap opera, complete with over-the-top declarations and exaggerated self-pity. But here's the thing: it's not helping anyone, least of all your relationship.

## How Dramatizing Minimizes the Actual Issue

When you pull the "I'm the worst person ever" card, you're not really apologizing—you're fishing for reassurance. Instead of focusing on the actual issue and the hurt you caused, you're turning the spotlight onto yourself. It's like saying, "Yes, I messed up, but let's talk about how awful I feel about it."

This kind of apology is a distraction tactic. It shifts the conversation away from the specific wrongdoing and turns it into a pity party. Instead of acknowledging your mistake and addressing the hurt, you're forcing the other person to comfort you. It's emotional manipulation 101, and it does nothing to solve the problem at hand.

## Why This Tactic Shifts the Focus from the Hurt Caused to Seeking Pity

By dramatizing your apology, you're effectively saying, "Let's stop talking about what I did wrong and start talking about how bad I feel." It's a sneaky way to avoid taking full responsibility. Instead of making amends, you're seeking validation that you're not a terrible person. Spoiler alert: everyone makes mistakes, but not everyone turns their apology into an audition for a tragic hero role.

This tactic is problematic because it doesn't offer genuine remorse or a path to healing. It's all about you and your feelings, rather than the feelings of the person you hurt. It's a self-centered move that leaves the other person feeling unheard and unsupported.

### I'm Sorry, But Remember When You...

Ah, the classic deflection technique: "I'm sorry, but remember when you...". This one is a real gem. It's like saying, "I'm sorry for what I did, but let's not forget you're no saint either." It's the conversational equivalent of throwing a grenade into a truce negotiation.

### The Destructive Impact of Deflecting Blame by Highlighting the Other Person's Faults

When you bring up the other person's mistakes during an apology, you're not actually apologizing. Instead, you're turning the tables and deflecting blame. It's like saying, "Sure, I messed up, but let's talk about how you messed up too." This tactic is destructive because it shifts the focus from your wrongdoing to their faults, effectively nullifying any chance of genuine reconciliation.

This approach is not just counterproductive; it's outright toxic. Instead of mending the relationship, you're reigniting old conflicts and reopening old wounds. It turns the apology into a battleground, where the goal is not to heal but to win points. Spoiler alert: nobody wins in this scenario.

### Why This Approach Escalates Conflict Instead of Resolving It

By deflecting blame, you're essentially saying, "My mistake is justified because you've made mistakes too." This not only invalidates the other person's feelings but also escalates the conflict. Instead of addressing the current issue, you're dragging up past grievances and creating a laundry list of complaints. It's like trying to put out a fire by throwing gasoline on it.

This tactic undermines the sincerity of your apology. The other person feels attacked rather than comforted, and the original issue gets buried under a pile of mutual accusations. It's a fast track to a full-blown argument and does nothing to foster understanding or forgiveness.

### I Already Said Sorry... Why Aren't You Over It?

Here's another gem from the vault of terrible apologies: "I already said sorry... why aren't you over it?" This one is like saying, "I've done my part, now hurry up and get over your feelings." It's a masterclass in impatience and a surefire way to show just how little you actually care about resolving the issue.

### How Impatience Undermines the Sincerity of an Apology

When you apologize, it's not just about uttering the words "I'm sorry." It's about giving the other person the space and time they need to process their feelings and heal. Rushing them to get over it is like putting a band-aid on a deep wound and expecting it to heal instantly. Spoiler alert: it won't.

Impatience in an apology shows a lack of genuine remorse. It's like saying, "I've checked the apology box, now let's move on." This attitude invalidates the other person's emotions and minimizes the impact of your actions. Instead of demonstrating understanding and empathy, it comes across as self-centered and dismissive.

### The Importance of Giving the Other Person Time to Heal

Healing takes time, and everyone processes hurt differently. Some wounds take longer to heal than others, and that's okay. When you apologize, you're opening the door to reconciliation, but you can't rush someone through it. They need to walk through it at their own pace.

By showing patience, you're demonstrating that you respect their feelings and are committed to making things right. It's not just about saying "I'm sorry" but about proving through your actions that you're willing to give them the time and support they need to heal. This builds trust and shows that you genuinely care about their well-being.

### I'm Sorry for Whatever I Did

Ah, the delightfully vague apology: "I'm sorry for whatever I did." This one is the equivalent of throwing a wet blanket over a fire—completely ineffective and a little insulting. It's like saying, "I know I did something wrong, but I'm not really interested in figuring out what it was."

### Why Vague Apologies Fail to Address the Specific Issue

When you apologize with, "I'm sorry for whatever I did," you're basically admitting that you have no clue what you did wrong. It's a half-hearted attempt to sweep the issue under the rug without actually addressing it. This kind of apology is frustrating because it shows a lack of effort and concern for the specific hurt you caused.

Vague apologies are a cop-out. They avoid the hard work of reflecting on your actions and understanding their impact. It's like saying, "I want this to be over, but I'm not willing to put in the effort to understand why you're upset." This approach doesn't resolve the issue; it just glosses over it, leaving the hurt to simmer under the surface.

### The Need for Clear and Specific Acknowledgment of the Wrongdoing

A genuine apology requires clear and specific acknowledgment of what you did wrong. It shows that you've taken the time to reflect on your actions and understand their impact. Specificity is crucial because it demonstrates that you're taking the issue seriously and are committed to making things right.

Instead of saying, "I'm sorry for whatever I did," take the time to figure out exactly what you did that caused hurt. Be precise in your apology: "I'm sorry for canceling our plans last minute and not considering how important this was to you." This kind of specificity shows that you recognize the specific hurt and are taking responsibility for it.

Clear and specific apologies build trust and show that you're genuinely remorseful. They pave the way for meaningful dialogue and healing. So, ditch the vagueness and get real. Your partner deserves more than a blanket apology—they deserve your full attention and effort in making things right. Trust me, it's the difference between a Band-Aid and real healing.

## Saying Sorry Over Text Message

Let's talk about the absolute worst way to apologize: over text message. Seriously, folks, if you think you can type out a quick "sorry" and slap a sad face emoji on it, you might as well send a carrier pigeon with a note saying, "I don't really care."

## Emotional Limitations of Text Messages

Text messages are great for quick updates, memes, and deciding what's for dinner. Apologizing? Not so much. When you text an apology, you miss out on all the crucial non-verbal cues that show you actually give a damn. No tone of voice, no facial expressions, no body language. It's like trying to perform a Shakespearean monologue through a sock puppet.

Your heartfelt "I'm sorry" comes off as flat as a pancake, leaving the recipient wondering if you're actually sorry or just sorry you got caught. And let's be real, the last thing you want is for your apology to sound like it was composed by a robot.

## Why There's No Emoji That Can Replace a Heartfelt Apology

Now, I know what you're thinking: "But emojis!" Yes, those cute little icons that supposedly convey every emotion under the sun. But here's the cold, hard truth: there is no emoji that can replace a heartfelt apology.

Throwing a sad face or a crying emoji at the end of your "sorry" doesn't magically infuse it with genuine remorse. It's like putting a Band-Aid on a bullet wound. Sure, it covers it up a bit, but it doesn't address the underlying damage. An emoji is not going to convey the depth of your regret or the sincerity of your feelings. It's just a tiny, pixelated cop-out.

Think about it: would you feel better if someone apologized in person, looking you in the eye, versus getting a text with a teary-eyed emoji? Exactly. There's no contest. Apologies need to be personal. They need to be real. So, the next time you're tempted to text your way out of a screw-up, put down the phone, and make the effort to apologize in person. Trust me, it's worth it. Plus, you get the added bonus of not looking like a complete tool. Win-win!

## Apology Hall of Shame

Welcome to the Apology Hall of Shame, where we showcase some of the most epic fails in the history of public apologies. This isn't just a walk of shame; it's a full-blown parade of cringeworthy, tone-deaf, and downright disastrous attempts at saying "I'm sorry." Grab your popcorn and settle in because we're about to dive deep into the world of apologies that missed the mark by a mile.

At the end of each chapter, we'll take you through an infamous incident that left the public shaking their heads in disbelief. Each entry will start with a recap of what went down—whether it was a corporate blunder, a political misstep, or a CEO putting his foot firmly in his mouth. We'll lay out the facts and set the stage for the apology that followed.

Next, we'll break down exactly what went wrong with the apology. Was it the classic non-apology apology? Maybe it was dripping with insincerity or filled with excuses. We'll dissect these apologies with the precision of a surgeon, highlighting the key missteps that turned a bad situation into a public relations nightmare.

But we won't just stop at pointing out the flaws. We'll also delve into the backlash that ensued. Public outrage, social media firestorms, and the long-lasting damage to reputations—these bad apologies didn't just fail to mend fences; they often poured gasoline on the fire. We'll explore the reactions and repercussions that followed these failed attempts at making amends.

And because we're not just here to criticize, we'll also offer some constructive advice. Each entry in the Apology Hall of Shame will include a "How It Could Have Been Done Better" section. We'll suggest how a sincere, well-crafted apology might have turned things around and possibly salvaged some dignity. After all, everyone makes mistakes, but how you handle them can make all the difference.

So, buckle up and prepare for a wild ride through the world of apologies gone wrong. At the end of each chapter, the Apology Hall of Shame will provide valuable lessons on what not to do and insights into how to get it right. Learn from the mistakes of others, one disastrous apology at a time.

# Apology Hall of Shame: Equifax Data Breach 2017

In September 2017, Equifax, one of the big three credit reporting agencies, dropped a bombshell. They announced that hackers had exploited a vulnerability in their website to access a treasure trove of personal data. We're talking names, social security numbers, birth dates, addresses, and even some driver's license numbers and credit card information. Basically, everything you'd need to steal someone's identity, charge up a fun little European trip in their name, and then vanish like the ghost of credit theft past.

But wait, it gets worse. The breach didn't just happen overnight. The hackers had been rummaging around in Equifax's systems from mid-May to July 2017. That's right, over two months of unfettered access while Equifax apparently had no clue. And when they finally did discover the breach in July, they waited until September to let the public know. Because who needs to rush these things, right?

## What They Did Wrong

Now, let's get to the apology—if you can even call it that. Equifax's initial response was a masterclass in how not to handle a crisis. Their CEO at the time, Richard Smith, issued a statement that was about as comforting as a wet blanket in a snowstorm. Let's take a look at the initial apology:

*"This is clearly a disappointing event for our company, and one that strikes at the heart of who we are and what we do. I apologize to consumers and our business customers for the concern and frustration this causes."*

Concern and frustration? Richard, people were on the verge of panic attacks over their stolen identities, and you're talking about frustration? Also can we examine this for a second: "disappointing event for our company?" What about the disappointing event for the people who actually had their identity stolen. Nobody cares about Equifax at a time like this, Mr. Smith.

The apology was seen as completely inadequate and insincere. It lacked empathy, urgency, and any real sense of taking responsibility. Equifax tried to offer free credit monitoring and identity theft protection services, but even that came with strings attached—like waiving your right to sue them. Talk about adding insult to injury.

## The Backlash

The backlash was immediate and fierce. Public outrage exploded, with everyone from individual consumers to state attorneys general demanding answers and accountability. Social media lit up with scathing comments and memes mocking Equifax's response. Congressional hearings followed, where Equifax executives were grilled like overcooked steaks.

Equifax's stock plummeted, lawsuits started piling up, and trust in the company hit rock bottom. The mishandling of the breach and the half-hearted apology didn't just damage Equifax's reputation—it obliterated it.

## How It Could Have Been Done Better

So, how could Equifax have handled this better? For starters, a genuine apology would have been nice along with some transparency and efforts to rectify the situation. Below is a quick draft that I was able to put together of what a better apology might have sounded like.

*We deeply regret the recent data breach that has compromised the personal information of millions of Americans. This is a devastating event that strikes at the very core of our commitment to safeguarding your data, and we are profoundly sorry for the distress and anxiety this incident has caused.*

*We want to be transparent about what happened and what we are doing to address the situation. On July 29th, we discovered that unauthorized access to our systems had occurred, resulting in the exposure of sensitive information, including names, social security numbers, birth dates, addresses, and, in some cases, driver's license numbers and credit card information. This breach is unacceptable, and we take full responsibility for the failure to protect your personal data.*

*Our immediate priority is to provide support and assistance to those affected. We are offering free credit monitoring and identity theft protection services to all U.S. consumers for one year, with no strings attached. You will not be required to waive any legal rights to access these services. We are also establishing a dedicated website and a call center to provide you with detailed information on how to protect yourself and your family.*

*We understand that an apology alone is not enough. Therefore, we are taking decisive action to enhance our security measures and prevent such incidents from happening again. We have engaged leading cybersecurity experts to conduct a thorough review of our systems and processes. We are implementing their recommendations immediately and will continue to invest in robust security technologies to safeguard your information.*

*We are committed to being fully transparent with you throughout this process. We will provide regular updates on our progress and the steps we are taking to rectify this situation. Our goal is to restore your trust in Equifax by demonstrating our dedication to your security and privacy.*

*We understand the gravity of this breach and the responsibility we have to you, our customers. We are here to answer your questions, address your concerns, and provide the support you need during this difficult time. Please contact us through our dedicated channels for any assistance.*

*Once again, we deeply apologize for this breach and the impact it has had on you. We are committed to making things right and to ensuring the security of your personal information in the future.*

4

# Why Saying Sorry is Harder Than Rocket Science

ALRIGHT, LET'S DIVE INTO why people absolutely blow at apologies. There are a bunch of reasons someone might be totally inept at offering a decent, genuine, and compassionate apology—the kind that everyone desperately wants when they feel wronged by someone they actually give a damn about.

Before we dive into the laundry list of emotional baggage that someone could be towing around that prevents them from uttering "I'm sorry" with power, let's understand why it's important to look at the root issues, and there are four reasons I can think of: Understanding the Underlying Emotions, Building Self-Awareness, Improving Communication, and Enhancing Emotional Intelligence.

## Understanding Underlying Emotions

If you can't figure out the underlying emotions at play, your apology is going to miss the mark like a drunk guy throwing darts. You might think you're apologizing for one thing, but the person you're apologizing to actually wants to hear something else entirely. It's like showing up to a costume party in a tuxedo—you look great, but you're still out of place.

Let's break it down. Say you break someone's vase. You think the right move is to say, "I'm sorry for breaking your vase." Sure, that's a start, but it's like bringing a knife to a gunfight. What the person really wants to hear is something deeper. Like, "I'm sorry an heirloom from your family is gone and you can't get it back. I realize that you probably feel like I don't care about your family's legacy, and that must be painful. That was not my intention, and I want to make this right."

See the difference? The first apology is superficial; it's about the object. The second digs into the real issue—the emotional pain and the feeling of disrespect. If you can tap into those underlying emotions, you're not just apologizing; you're showing that you actually give a damn about how the other person feels.

## Building Self-Awareness

Alright, let's get real. If you suck at apologizing, don't just ask, "How do I get better?" Ask, "Why do I suck so hard in the first place?" This isn't about learning to parrot the right words—it's about digging into the mess that is you. When you start unraveling why your apologies are as satisfying as a soggy sandwich, you begin unlocking secrets that make you a better human. And guess what? Better humans have way more fun.

Without self-awareness, your relationships will tank faster than a lead balloon, and you'll be left scratching your head, wondering what the hell went wrong. It's like stumbling around in the dark, bumping into crap, and then blaming the furniture for existing. Newsflash: therapy is a booming business because people are walking emotional train wrecks without a clue about their feelings or how to deal with them. Getting a grip on your own baggage solves 80% of these problems. Why wouldn't you want that?

Being unaware of your own emotional junk is like trying to navigate with a map written in Klingon. Spoiler alert: it's not going to end well. So, get to know yourself. Understand what sets you off and why you react like a lunatic sometimes. It's not just about upgrading your apologies—it's about not being a disaster in your relationships.

## Improving Communication

Whether you're looking for an apology or trying to give one, understanding the root issue of why it's hard for you or your partner to spit it out allows you to speak *directly* to the problem. No more playing detective, trying to figure out what the hell is really bothering everyone. You're no Sherlock Holmes and nobody's paying you to walk around with a magnifying glass and a deerstalker hat figuring out little riddles. Talking directly to the problem is how we cut through the crap and get straight to the point.

Communication is the smoking gun for keeping any relationship—romantic or otherwise—thriving. But here's the kicker: communication hinges on understanding what makes both you and the other person tick. What makes them happy, sad, angry? What triggers their inner Hulk or makes them curl up like a hedgehog?

Without this understanding, you're just two people talking past each other, like a bad comedy routine. It's like trying to have a conversation with someone in a language you don't speak, except instead of hilarity, it's just frustration and resentment. So, do yourself a favor and get to know the emotional landscape. What are the triggers and traumas at play here?

When you can speak to these issues directly, you're not just communicating—you're connecting. And that connection is the secret sauce that makes relationships work. No more guessing games, no more walking on eggshells. Just honest, direct communication that hits the mark. Because at the end of the day, that's what keeps the ship sailing smoothly, without crashing into every iceberg along the way.

## Enhancing Emotional Intelligence

If you're reading this book, I'm assuming you have at least a tiny spark of desire to improve yourself. Sure, this is a relationship book, but let's be real—it's also a self-improvement book. We love to yammer on about diet, exercise, and making bank until we're blue in the face, but we often skip over building our emotional intelligence. And here's the kicker: EQ isn't just as important as IQ—it's estimated that 80% of your success in life depends on it.

Think about it. What's business without understanding the emotional motivations of your partners and affiliates? A soulless transaction that has a tendency to be a one-and-done deal instead of a lifelong partnership. And what's a diet worth if you can't grasp the reasons behind wanting to shed those pounds? Understanding whether your goal is healthy and sustainable is key to making it stick.

By getting to the bottom of why you or your partner struggle with apologies, you start to unlock the core components of human behavior. You begin to see what makes people tick, what drives their actions, and how emotions play into every decision. The tangential benefit? All apologies become easier to give and receive across all your relationships. It's like upgrading from dial-up to fiber optic—everything just works better, faster, and smoother.

So, boost that emotional intelligence and understand the why behind the struggle. Not only will your apologies improve, but your entire life will get richer and more fulfilling. Enriching your Emotional intelligence is like ordering from the secret menu when it comes to success, happiness, and not being the emotional equivalent of a brick wall.

Let's now dive into the list of emotional roadblocks that act like concrete-reinforced brick walls on the road to effective apologies. Again, not only does it help if you find you have one of these walls up, it helps your partner too.

If your partner is the one who breaks out in hives and throws a temper tantrum anytime the thought of an apology arises, you'll understand which one of these excuses they're hiding behind, and you can throw them a bone. If they're missing a piece of the puzzle, you can hand it to them, making it easier for them to give you the kind of apology you're after. Seriously, that's a heck of a gift, right?

## Fear of Admitting Fault

The first big roadblock? The fear of admitting fault. It's like people think saying "I screwed up" is going to cause the apocalypse.

This fear of admitting fault can come from all sorts of places. Picture this: you've got someone who's been in trouble with the law. If there's even a hint of legal implications, you can bet your bottom dollar they're not going to admit fault. During mediations, there's this massive fear of fessing up because the consequences are real and scary. So you've got to ask yourself, what's the reaction they're dreading? What terrifying outcome are they trying to dodge by refusing to admit they messed up?

Usually in relationships the biggest fear to admitting fault is that the relationship vanishes like a donut at a police station. If you can let them know that you'll still stand by their side, even if they did the bad thing they're denying or refusing to accept accountability for, it might help this hurdle start to crumble.

## Avoiding Weakness

Then there are the folks who just don't want to look weak. Take my client, for example, who grew up as one of ten kids. In that family, admitting you did something wrong was like waving a flag saying, "Punish me!" The second you apologized, you were in trouble. So the kids learned to shift blame faster than a politician during an election year. Imagine the chaos of ten kids, right? Parents don't have the time to play detective and figure out who stole the last cookie or who didn't do their chores. If someone fessed up, it made things easier. Maybe the punishment was lighter, but the guilty party still got grounded, while the rest of the kids got off scot-free.

Even when someone knows they're wrong, the act of apologizing has this looming consequence that's totally at odds with what they want. You've got to figure out what that is. For someone like my client, it's a pattern ingrained since childhood: admitting fault equals showing weakness. In other cases, admitting fault means being wrong, and wearing that "I'm wrong" label is about as comfortable as a wool sweater in the Sahara.

### The Need to Always Be Right

And why is it so crucial to always be right? Seriously, a lot of couples have either a husband or a wife who just can't stand being wrong. You've got to dig deeper and ask, why is it so hard to admit being wrong? I mean, I'm wrong all the time. It's human. It's okay. I even like being wrong sometimes. It takes the pressure off of feeling like I have to be right—but maybe that's just me.

For some people, being wrong might feel like an existential crisis. It's like, if they're wrong, you won't love them anymore. Or maybe it messes with their whole sense of self. Their identity is so wrapped up in being right, and that's just not healthy. This need to always be right often stems from deep-rooted insecurities and a fear of vulnerability. It can be a defense mechanism to protect their self-esteem and sense of identity. Admitting they're wrong can feel like a direct threat to their self-worth, so they cling to being right to maintain a façade of competence and perfection.

Insisting on being right can also be about control and power, giving them a sense of superiority and security. It helps avoid the discomfort of cognitive dissonance, where conflicting ideas cause mental stress. For some, it's a learned behavior from an environment where mistakes were harshly punished, leading to a habit of always striving to be right for self-protection. Lacking self-awareness, they might not even realize their need to be right, while others seek validation and approval, proving themselves right to gain recognition and affirm their worth.

Understanding these motivations can help in addressing the behavior and fostering healthier communication and relationships.

## Fear of Rejection

This ties into another big reason people suck at apologies: the fear of rejection. It's not just about the consequences or backlash; it's about being afraid that if they admit fault, they'll be rejected. If I yell at you and then apologize, I'm admitting I was wrong. But what if that means I made an unforgivable mistake? What if you reject me as a friend, a partner? That fear of rejection is real and intense.

If you're constantly afraid of being rejected by your partner, your relationship is on shaky ground. You need to build—or rebuild—trust. Here's a pro tip: before demanding an apology, offer some reassurance. Say something like, "I need an apology, but know that we're staying together. I love you and accept you for who you are, but my feelings are hurt, and I need you to acknowledge that."

By doing this, you're taking the fear of rejection off the table. You're creating a safe space for your partner to own up to their mistakes without fearing they'll lose you. And that's how you get a real, meaningful apology.

## Embarrassment and Shame

Another reason people are terrible at apologizing is embarrassment and shame. Let's be real—no one likes feeling remorse. It's uncomfortable. Apologizing can feel like you're walking barefoot over Legos. It sucks. But getting through that shame and embarrassment makes you a stronger person. You can even coach your partner through it.

Embarrassment is that lovely feeling when you realize you've royally screwed up, and now the universe has front-row seats to your personal humiliation. Picture Greg, who thought his sarcasm was top-tier comedy until his wife, Lisa, had enough. The second she called him out, Greg's face turned the shade of an overripe tomato. Instead of manning up, Greg decided to play the "You're too sensitive" card. Why? Because admitting he messed up felt like stripping naked in Times Square. It's easier to pretend you're right than to own up and face the cringe.

Then there's shame, embarrassment's evil twin. If embarrassment is tripping in public, shame is believing you're the clumsy idiot who'll never walk straight. Emily, for example, completely blanked on her husband Jack's birthday. When Jack expressed his hurt, Emily didn't just feel bad—she felt like a rotten human being. Her brain went into overdrive: "I'm the worst partner ever. How could I forget?" This kind of self-flagellation makes you want to curl up in a ball and hope the earth swallows you whole. Admitting fault when you're drowning in shame feels like adding a cherry on top of your humiliation sundae.

## Pride and Ego

Ever notice how saying "I'm sorry" feels like performing open-heart surgery on yourself without anesthesia? Yeah, it's that bad. Pride and ego are the surgeons, and they've got the shakiest hands in the business. Let's break down why your inner diva and tyrant make you allergic to apologizing.

Apologizing is like handing over the TV remote in the middle of your favorite show. Ego hates that. It's got a white-knuckle grip on the control panel of your life. Giving it up? Unthinkable. You'd rather eat a raw onion than let someone else dictate the narrative. Your ego screams, "If I apologize, I lose control!" And nobody, especially your ego, wants to admit they can't handle that loss.

There are also power dynamics to think of when it comes to pride and ego. Apologies in power dynamics are like inviting a rookie to your poker table and losing to them on the first hand. If you're the boss, the parent, or the alpha dog in any situation, saying sorry feels like surrendering your crown. You're the big cheese, the head honcho, the one who calls the shots. Apologizing? That's for peons! Your pride says, "Keep the upper hand at all costs!" and before you know it, you're doubling down on your mistake instead of owning it.

Imagine walking through a cactus patch barefoot while confessing your worst secrets on live TV. That's the emotional ride of an apology. Shame, guilt, and embarrassment roll in like an unwanted ex at a family reunion. Your pride jumps in to save face, saying, "Abort mission! This is a cringe-fest!" Your ego isn't interested in this emotional rollercoaster, preferring to ghost the situation instead of facing it head-on.

So next time you feel that lump in your throat when it's time to apologize, just remember: It's not you. It's your diva pride and tyrant ego throwing a tantrum. Recognizing their tricks can help you navigate through the apology minefield with a bit more finesse and a lot less drama.

## Lack of Understanding

There are also those who genuinely don't understand what they did wrong. Maybe the person they offended is more sensitive than they are. They might think, "What are you complaining about? I don't get it." This cluelessness can be toxic to a relationship. You need to explain that some people are more sensitive about certain things. I once worked with a religious couple who had strict rules and regulations. Their family members, who were unaware of these practices, inadvertently caused offense. This lack of understanding can be a huge barrier.

## Belief That the Apology Won't Be Accepted

Here's another curveball: the fear that your apology will get rejected like a bad Tinder date. If you're thinking, "Why bother? They won't accept it anyway," you're setting yourself up for a self-imposed purgatory. You hope things will magically get better over time, but newsflash: they won't. This mindset screams, "I have zero faith in the power of apologies," and it's a pretty bleak view of your partner. If you're convinced your husband won't accept your apology, you're not giving him a fair shake. Everyone is capable of accepting a sincere apology when it's done right. Want proof? There are still Jews living in Germany today.

If you think your apology will crash and burn, it's time to have a chat. Tell your partner, "I'm ready to accept your apology if it's genuine and heartfelt." Make apologies a normal part of your relationship because, spoiler alert, we're all human and screw up sometimes. Build that mutual understanding and respect for the art of the apology.

But let's flip the script. If you're not ready to hear an apology, shut it down before it starts. If my wife came at me after pulling some major stunt and I wasn't in the mood to forgive, I'd cut her off mid-sentence. She'd start with, "I want to tell you about—" and I'd hit pause. "Hold up. I want to hear your apology, but I'm not ready yet. Give me some time." That's not just fair; it's necessary. If this happens and your partner asks, "How much time?" just say, "Check in with me tomorrow," or "Give me an hour." It's all about setting the stage for when you're both ready to handle it like adults.

## Fear of Damaging Reputation

Now, let's scale this up. If it's a newer relationship, or a more public one—like something at work or in a big family—there's a fear of damaging your reputation that comes with an apology. And that's a legit fear, especially if your business or social standing relies on people thinking you're flawless. The fear of tarnishing that reputation and the fallout that comes with it is real. So, what do you do? Apologize in private, make sure it doesn't get out, and maybe even question if your reputation is as fragile as you think.

## Feeling That the Other Person Is at Fault

Now, let's hit the real kicker: the glorious feeling that it's entirely the other person's fault. This happens all the time. Someone's like, "Why should I apologize? They should be apologizing to me!" Welcome to super dangerous territory, my friend. In relationships, both parties usually screw up in some way. If I yell at you because you burned the toast and the kitchen got smoky, sure, you should apologize for nearly torching the house, but I shouldn't have lost my cool either.

Here's the thing: if someone reacts calmly and compassionately—like if my wife almost burns the house down and I go, "Oh my God, are you okay? Is everything safe?"—you'll probably get an apology without even asking for it.

Compassion is like a magic wand that summons apologies. If my kid hits me while roughhousing and I calmly say, "Ow, that hurt," they'll apologize. But if I snap, "What the hell are you thinking?" they'll go on the defense faster than a cat in a dog park: "Well, you were roughhousing too!"

So, next time you think it's all their fault, take a beat. Show some compassion, and watch how apologies flow without needing to drag them out kicking and screaming.

## Fear of Vulnerability

Some folks hate being open and exposed, like admitting fault is the emotional equivalent of stripping down in public and yelling, "Here are all my flaws!" It's scarier than your mom deciding to follow you on Instagram. Being vulnerable means being brave, and if someone can't handle that exposed, unknown space, it's tough.

You've got to step up and say, "Look, I'm going to be vulnerable with you. I don't know how you'll react, but I'm apologizing because it's the right thing to do, and you deserve it...and if you have any human decency in your heart you will be gentle with me." Okay, maybe skip that last part about human decency. That was a bit much but you get the point.

If the person on the other side is the one struggling with it, you need to lay it out: "Listen, you've got to be vulnerable and apologize. You don't know how I'm going to react, and that's what relationships are all about. We face the unknown for each other and see what happens."

If you're not willing to show me your flaws and trust that I'll accept you, warts and all, then what are you doing in this relationship? If you can't be vulnerable with me, who can you be vulnerable with? The Roomba? I know it's better than doing house chores than most of us, but come on, man! These emotional obstacles to apologizing are the biggies. There might be more, but these are the ones that trip people up the most.

**Overcoming These Obstacles**

Identify which of the obstacles we discussed are the ones you're struggling with. Determine which ones your partner is facing. Talk about these obstacles either before or after the apology to make it easier next time. You'll find that addressing the root issue directly makes the process easier over time.

# Apology Hall of Shame:
# United Airlines 2017

In this chapter, we're not just gawking at a public apology train wreck—we're diving into the messy guts behind it. We've covered the why behind crappy apologies, so let's put that knowledge to use. Time to escape theory-land and see how it all crashes and burns in the real world.

Let's rewind to April 9, 2017, when United Airlines decided to turn a routine overbooked flight into a scene straight out of an action movie. The star? Dr. David Dao, a 69-year-old passenger who had the audacity to think his ticket actually guaranteed him a seat - imagine that. United, needing to make room for their crew members, asked for volunteers to give up their seats. When no one raised their hand, they went full Gestapo and randomly selected passengers to be "re-accommodated."

Dr. Dao refused to give up his seat, citing his need to see patients the next day. Instead of understanding that a doctor might need to, you know, doctor, United called in airport security. What followed was a violent altercation where Dr. Dao was dragged down the aisle, bloodied and screaming. This isn't hyperbole either, he sustained a concussion, a broken nose, the loss of two front teeth, and significant damage to a his sinuses that required reconstructive surgery. Passengers whipped out their phones, capturing the brutal scene that would soon go viral and turn United Airlines into a global pariah.

## The Failed Apology

Enter Oscar Munoz, United's CEO, who decided to throw gasoline on this PR dumpster fire. His initial response was a masterclass in how not to apologize. Here's the full statement in all its tone-deaf glory:

"This is an upsetting event to all of us here at United. I apologize for having to re-accommodate these customers. Our team is moving with a sense of urgency to work with the authorities and conduct our own detailed review of what happened. We are also reaching out to this passenger to talk directly to him and further address and resolve this situation."

Wow, Oscar. You really nailed the "blame the victim" approach. First, there's the phrase "re-accommodate," which sounds like you're offering a first-class upgrade rather than forcibly removing someone. I wonder if they're going to reclassify assault and battery anytime soon to "re-accommodating" on the judicial level. Second, there's zero acknowledgment of the violence inflicted upon Dr. Dao. That apology sounds like someone misplaced a bunch of passwords, not like a 69-year-old doctor got his nose broken.

## The Public Backlash

As you can imagine, the public reaction was akin to a digital lynch mob. Social media exploded with outrage, memes, and calls to boycott United. The company's stock plummeted, losing nearly $1 billion in market value within a day. The hashtag #BoycottUnited trended worldwide, and even celebrities joined in the condemnation. United's brand was dragged through the mud, and Oscar Munoz was in the crosshairs.

## The Emotional Core

Let's examine now the root and emotional core behind the crap apology applying what we went over in this chapter.

## Fear of Admitting fault

Munoz's first move? Blame the victim. Instead of owning up, he implied Dr. Dao was at fault. Because, obviously, a 69-year-old man would choose to get his nose broken and teeth knocked out for fun. Admitting fault would've been like stepping on a legal and reputational landmine, and Munoz wasn't about to play that game.

## Avoiding Weakness

Corporate bigwigs hate showing weakness like cats hate water. Munoz avoided fully admitting United's error because, in the corporate world, admitting you messed up is like flashing a neon sign saying, "I'm weak!" Instead, he shifted blame to keep that façade of invincibility intact.

## Pride and Ego

Munoz's ego probably wrote the apology. Apologizing unconditionally might've felt like stripping naked on live TV—his pride couldn't handle it. So, he clung to control and avoided a full mea culpa, keeping his dignity bruised but not shattered.

## Fear of Damaging Reputation

Munoz likely thought that admitting fault would tarnish United's shiny corporate image even more. His defensive stance screamed, "Let's hope this blows over if we just downplay it!" Spoiler alert: it didn't. The public saw right through it, and the backlash was savage.

## Belief That the Apology Won't Be Accepted

Munoz might have figured that a genuine apology would be like throwing a band-aid on a bullet wound—useless. So, instead of risking an apology that might not be accepted, he tried to control the damage with a half-assed non-apology.

In summary, Munoz's initial "apology" was a masterclass in cowardice: fear of admitting fault, dodging weakness, pride, and ego on full display, fear of ruining United's reputation, and thinking a real apology wouldn't fly. The result? An apology that blamed the victim and took zero responsibility. Bravo, Munoz. Bravo.

## How the Apology Could Have Been Better

If you throw aside all of those emotional self-preservation tactics that made the apology wreak like a month-old fish you forgot in the fridge, here's what that apology might have looked like:

*Dear Passengers and United Customers,*

*We are deeply sorry for the violent and traumatic incident involving Dr. David Dao on Flight 3411. This was a disgraceful event, and we are fully responsible. Dr. Dao was subjected to treatment that no human being should ever endure, and for that, we apologize unreservedly.*

*Effective immediately, we are conducting a thorough review of our procedures for handling overbooked situations. We are committed to ensuring that such an incident never occurs again. We are reaching out to Dr. Dao to provide a sincere, personal apology and substantial compensation to cover his medical expenses and emotional distress.*

*We understand that actions speak louder than words, and we are committed to earning back your trust through concrete changes and improved policies.*

And just to sprinkle a little something extra, how about offering a free flight to any destination valid for a whole year to everyone who witnessed that horror show on the plane? It's not just about saying sorry; it's about showing you mean it.

The easiest thing to do would have been to offer someone a thousand dollars to voluntarily leave the plane. No takers? Two thousand plus hotel accommodations for the evening. No takers? Five thousand. You're telling me for five thousand dollars there wasn't a single person on that airplane that wouldn't have minded staying in Chicago instead of flying to Louisville for one more day? Heck, I think I would have paid you to let me stay in Chicago for an extra day if my destination was Louisville. Nothing against Louisville but have you ever had a Chicago hot dog? Those little tomato slices and poppy seed bun - delicious!

Even if United had to spend fifty thousand dollars bumping ten passengers off the flight to re-accommodate peacefully it's a drop in the bucket compared to the billion-dollar nose dive their stock took. The policy they should have been looking at is the overbooking policy so this incident doesn't happen again.

# 5

# Facepalm Moments: Recognizing and Owning Your Mistakes

WHILE I'M GOING TO outline the several steps of a great apology, I want you to know that this isn't some tall mountain you have to climb. Think of it like learning to ride a bike: at first, you're wobbling all over the place, maybe crashing into a few bushes, but eventually, you're cruising down the street without a second thought. Apologizing with grace and sincerity becomes second nature over time. Sure, you might occasionally still fall off and land on your ego, but hey, that's part of the process.

Even if it's not second nature just yet, don't sweat it. Delivering a great apology doesn't require a marathon effort. In fact, all the steps can be done in a matter of minutes, sometimes even seconds. We're not talking about drafting a treaty here. Just a few moments of genuine reflection and expression can work wonders. And let's be real—most people just want to hear you acknowledge you screwed up without dragging it out like a daytime soap opera.

## The First Step: Recognition

The first step of the process is recognition. You have to know what you're apologizing for, or else it's just empty words. Imagine someone hands you an award, but you have no clue what it's for—kind of loses its meaning, right? It's the same with apologies. You need to pinpoint exactly what you did wrong.

This is why when we teach toddlers to apologize, we don't just accept the half-hearted "sorry" mumbled with all the enthusiasm of a teenager being asked to clean their room. We follow up with, "What are you sorry for?" It's the same principle here. If you don't know what you did, how can you make amends?

So, take a moment to reflect and recognize your mistake. It's a bit like finding a needle in a haystack—only in this case, the needle is your blunder and the haystack is your day-to-day life. Once you've identified it, you're already on the path to delivering a genuine apology.

## The Two Places all These Ideas Come From

Before we get too far into the nitty-gritty of recognizing your goofs, let's take a little detour and explore the origins of these apology steps. It's not like I woke up one day, channeled my inner Dr. Phil, and declared myself the apology guru. No, these steps are rooted in wisdom much older and more profound than my own ramblings. They've been shaped and refined over centuries, drawing from sources that know a thing or two about human relationships and the art of saying sorry.

There are two places where I draw my inspiration for effective apologies. The first source is the Torah, the Jewish Bible. Now, you might be thinking, "What does an ancient religious text have to do with my modern-day screw-ups?" Quite a lot, actually. The Torah is a treasure trove of wisdom on human behavior, accountability, and making things right. It's filled with stories of people messing up, owning their mistakes, and seeking forgiveness. If you think your blunders are unique, trust me, the folks in the Torah have been there, done that, and probably got a few stone tablets to prove it.

And in case you don't know much about me, I'm a pretty religious Jew and I was technically a rabbi before I was a counselor. Just to clarify I did a few weddings, funerals, and delivered a couple of sermons but I was a pinch hitter at best as you might be able to tell by my unflinching sarcastic tone in this book. My Jewish faith is pretty integral to my outlook on life in general so it should act as no surprise that it is integral to my views on apologies and relationships as a whole. However, I don't want you to feel like this book was a bait and switch so rest assured that this is not going to be a deep dive into God, spirituality or anything woo-woo.

The second source of inspiration comes from my practice as a couples counselor. Over the years, I've helped countless couples navigate the rocky terrain of marital discord, and a big part of that journey involves mastering the art of apologizing. My approach blends three powerful frameworks: The Gottman Method, Attachment Theory, and Imago Therapy.

**A Little More About the Clinical Stuff**

The Gottman Method, developed by Drs. John and Julie Gottman, is all about understanding and improving communication patterns within relationships. It emphasizes the importance of recognizing and validating your partner's feelings—a crucial component of a meaningful apology.

Attachment Theory delves into how our early relationships with caregivers shape our interactions as adults. It's like the psychological version of "blame it on your parents," but with more nuance. Understanding attachment styles can help you see why you and your partner react the way you do during conflicts and, more importantly, how to apologize in a way that resonates with them.

Imago Therapy, created by Harville Hendrix and Helen LaKelly Hunt, focuses on the idea that we subconsciously seek partners who reflect unresolved issues from our childhood. It's like Freud's greatest hits but with more emphasis on healing and connection. This approach teaches us to recognize and address these deeper issues when we apologize, making our amends more profound and transformative.

In fact, if you are looking for a counselor to help you with apologizing during a therapy session, I would look for someone with experience as an Imago therapist as they will jump into this work more so than just about any other couples therapist you will find.

By combining these rich sources of wisdom—the Torah's timeless teachings and the modern psychological frameworks from my counseling/coaching practice—we get a holistic approach to apologies. One that's grounded in ancient principles and backed by contemporary research. So, when I talk about recognizing your mistakes, know that it's not just some pop psychology fluff. It's a step that's been vetted by sages and scholars alike.

## Some Brief Background On the God Stuff

While this book is not a spiritual one by definition, I personally believe that all human interaction has a spiritual component. Whether we acknowledge it or not, there's an underlying depth to our connections that transcends the everyday bickering over who forgot to take out the trash. I feel a duty to explain the sources of my approach in case you want to dig deeper for yourself. Knowing where these concepts come from can enrich your understanding and perhaps even offer you new perspectives on your own relationships.

While there are several passages in the actual written Torah (Hebrew Bible) that mention repentance, the two sources I have leaned on the most are commentaries on the Torah. The first is the Talmud, which records the Jewish Oral Law. Specifically, Talmud Bavli, Yoma 86b. This passage in the Gemara delves into fascinating discussions about repentance.

In this section, you'll find debates and insights from ancient rabbis who were basically the original relationship experts, long before we had reality TV shows telling us how to find love. They didn't just scratch the surface; they dug deep into the human psyche, exploring the nuances of what it means to genuinely repent and seek forgiveness. Their discussions range from the straightforward to the philosophical, offering a rich tapestry of wisdom on how to truly recognize and rectify our wrongs.

The wisdom found in these texts can be incredibly relevant today. They remind us that the act of apologizing is more than just saying "I'm sorry." It's about understanding the impact of our actions, acknowledging our mistakes with sincerity, and making a genuine effort to change. These ancient teachings provide a solid foundation for the steps outlined in this book, ensuring that they are not just practical but also profoundly meaningful.

One fascinating thought discussed is that the idea of repentance was created before the formation of the earth. Yep, you heard that right—before there were trees, oceans, or even gravity, there was the concept of "my bad." Now, I don't want to dive into a deep philosophical discussion here about what that means on a spiritual level, but just imagine for a moment: the universe's grand blueprint included a built-in feature for apologizing and making amends.

It's like the cosmic engineers were sitting around, drafting the plans for existence, and one of them said, "Hey, before we get into this whole 'light' and 'darkness' thing, shouldn't we address what happens when people inevitably screw up?" And thus, the idea of repentance was born, nestled comfortably in the fabric of reality before physical matter even made its debut.

For Jewish culture, this isn't just a fun fact to toss around at dinner parties (though it does make for great conversation). It's evidence that the idea of apologizing and forgiveness is so deeply intertwined with the purpose of the world that it was a foundational element. So, next time you feel a bit reluctant to apologize, remember: it's literally in the universe's DNA. You're not just making amends—you're fulfilling a cosmic destiny!

Okay, maybe that's a bit of an exaggeration, but the point stands: the importance of recognizing our mistakes and seeking forgiveness is woven into the very essence of our existence. So, don't shy away from it. Embrace it, and know that in doing so, you're participating in a tradition that's as old as time itself.

The second source is from Maimonides, one of the lead commentators of the Jewish Bible. If you've never heard of him, Maimonides (or Rambam, as he's often called) was basically the ultimate multi-hyphenate: a rabbi, physician, philosopher, and all-around smarty pants. Think of him as the medieval version of a Renaissance man who, instead of dabbling in painting or sculpture, mastered the art of life advice.

If you'd like to dig deeper into Maimonides' work, you can look up Rambam, Hilchot Teshuva. There, you'll find the sources for much of what we'll discuss about apologies and repentance. Rambam didn't just offer vague suggestions; he laid out a clear, step-by-step guide on how to recognize and atone for our mistakes.

His work is like the ancient equivalent of a "How to Apologize for Dummies" book, but with way more gravitas and fewer cartoons. Maimonides breaks down the process of teshuva (repentance) into actionable steps, making it accessible and practical for anyone seeking to make things right.

So, while I may be adding a dash of humor and a sprinkle of sarcasm to the mix, know that the foundations of these apology steps are rooted in centuries-old wisdom. Maimonides' insights provide a robust framework that not only helps us navigate the tricky waters of apologizing but also adds depth and meaning to our efforts.

Feel free to explore his work if you want to get the full, unfiltered version from the master himself. Just be prepared for some dense reading—Maimonides didn't pull any punches when it came to depth and detail!

The last thing I'll say about apologizing and repentance as a Jew is that it's integral to our religion, and nowhere is this more evident than in some of our holidays. Take the Jewish New Year, Rosh Hashanah, for example. It's not just about eating apples dipped in honey and hoping for a sweet year ahead. No, Rosh Hashanah is the ultimate annual performance review, where God decides who among us will live and who will die that year. Talk about high stakes!

Rosh Hashanah is a day of judgment, and the core theme is to evaluate where you stand in the world mentally, emotionally, and spiritually. It's like a cosmic check-up, where you take stock of your life and try to mend the things that are broken. Did you snap at your coworker over a petty disagreement? Did you forget your partner's birthday (again)? Now's the time to own up to those slip-ups.

The process of apologizing and repentance is woven into the fabric of this holiday, and it's where many of these laws and principles come from. It's about taking a moment to reflect on your actions, recognize your mistakes, and make a genuine effort to set things right. So if you're Jewish, when you're sitting in synagogue, reflecting on your year, and trying not to nod off during the rabbi's sermon, remember that this is your chance to hit the reset button on your life.

In essence, Rosh Hashanah is like the ultimate reboot for your soul. It's a time to clean up your act and start fresh, armed with the knowledge of what you did wrong and a plan to make amends. If you think about it, it's a pretty powerful concept. And if you can master the art of apologizing during this time, you're not just improving your relationships—you're aligning yourself with the very essence of what it means to live a meaningful life.

We even have a tradition as Jews to apologize to the people in our lives around this time of year and ask for forgiveness from each other. It's like a pre-emptive strike against grudges and lingering resentments. Imagine it as a seasonal house cleaning, but instead of dusting off shelves and vacuuming under the couch, you're tidying up your relationships.

As the High Holy Days approach, you might find Jews everywhere making awkward phone calls or sending heartfelt texts. "Hey, remember that time I borrowed your favorite shirt and spilled wine on it? My bad." Or, "I know I said some pretty unkind things during that heated Monopoly game last Hanukkah. I'm really sorry." It's all about clearing the air and making peace.

This tradition emphasizes the importance of face-to-face (or emoji-to-emoji) apologies. It's one thing to whisper a quick "sorry" to yourself or in prayer, but it's another to look someone in the eye and acknowledge your mistakes. It's a humbling experience, but it's also incredibly liberating. Plus, it saves you from the potential awkwardness of sitting next to someone in synagogue while both of you pretend that you didn't just have a massive blow-up over something trivial.

So, during this time of year, you might see Jews taking a deep breath, swallowing their pride, and reaching out to mend fences. It's not always easy, but it's a vital part of our tradition. It's like hitting the reset button on our relationships, ensuring we start the new year with a clean slate and a lighter heart.

Furthermore, just ten days after the new year, we have another holiday, Yom Kippur. This is where our fate for the year is sealed. It's like the final exam after a whirlwind course in self-reflection and repentance. I've always taken two messages from the fact that this holiday is only ten days apart from Rosh Hashanah.

First, even God knows you're going to screw up your apology and need a second chance to get it right. Think of it as a divine grace period. You've got ten days to reflect, realize that maybe your first attempt at saying sorry was more "oops" than heartfelt apology, and try again. It's like God is saying, "I know you tried, but let's give it another go, shall we?"

Second, you shouldn't wait too long to make something wrong right. If Yom Kippur was a month or two away from Rosh Hashanah, you'd probably get complacent. You'd start to rationalize, "Oh, I've got time. I'll apologize later," and before you know it, you're back to your old ways, and the whole point of Rosh Hashanah would be moot. The wounds would reopen, and your initial apology would lose its impact, essentially making you start from scratch.

Yom Kippur's placement reminds us that timeliness is key in mending relationships. The short span between the holidays creates a sense of urgency and reinforces the importance of prompt action. It's like a built-in deadline to ensure you don't procrastinate on the important stuff. After all, nobody wants to carry the baggage of unresolved issues into the new year.

So, these back-to-back holidays act as a powerful one-two punch for personal growth and reconciliation. They encourage us to take our apologies seriously, to recognize our mistakes swiftly, and to make amends promptly. It's a system designed to help us keep our relationships in good health, ensuring that we don't let our missteps fester and cause more harm over time. And let's face it, having a clear conscience and lighter heart as you move into the new year? Totally worth the effort.

## Now Let's Get Back to Recognition

The first step is defining the wrong done. This is what the Rambam calls "Hakarat HaChet": recognizing and acknowledging the specific wrongdoing. Now, I know this might sound like a no-brainer, but you'd be amazed at how often people bungle this step. It's not just about saying, "Yeah, I messed up." You need to get into the nitty-gritty details of what you did wrong. Think of it as painting a full picture of your misdeed, not just sketching a vague outline.

For example, did you scratch your wife's car, or did you scratch your wife's brand new car that she's been looking forward to getting for three months and was her most prized possession? There's a world of difference between those two statements. The first one sounds like an "oops" moment; the second one acknowledges the full gravity of your blunder. It's the difference between "I accidentally knocked over a vase" and "I knocked over the heirloom vase that's been in your family for generations and has sentimental value beyond measure."

Getting specific shows that you truly understand the impact of your actions. It's not enough to vaguely admit fault; you need to demonstrate that you've taken the time to think about what you did and why it matters. Saying, "I'm sorry I was late" is one thing, but saying, "I'm sorry I was late to our anniversary dinner, which made you feel unimportant and ruined an evening you had been looking forward to" is a whole different ball game.

So, when you're owning up to your mistakes, channel your inner detail-oriented detective. Pinpoint exactly what you did and why it matters. It's a crucial step in making your apology meaningful and sincere. Plus, it shows the person you wronged that you're not just trying to brush it off with a generic "my bad." You're genuinely committed to understanding and addressing the specific ways you've caused harm. And trust me, that goes a long way in the apology department.

## What is the Root Cause?

Next, let's talk about the importance of pinpointing the exact action that caused harm. This isn't just about acknowledging the aftermath of your screw-up; it's about understanding what you did to cause the damage in the first place. Were you texting while driving? Did you skip lunch, get hangry, and snap at your partner? Identifying the root cause of your actions is crucial for a meaningful apology.

Consider this: "I'm sorry I made you feel bad" is a pretty weak apology. It's like saying, "I'm sorry it rained on your parade," as if the hurt feelings magically appeared out of nowhere. Instead, you need to dig deeper. What did you do to make them feel bad? Were you not paying attention during an important conversation because you were glued to your phone? Did you forget an important date because you were too busy binge-watching your favorite show? (side note - they can always find this out by logging into your Netflix account so don't try to hide this).

Getting specific helps you understand and address the real issue. It's not just about the broken vase; it's about why the vase got broken in the first place. Were you being careless, rushing around without thinking, or perhaps you were frustrated and took it out on the nearest inanimate object? Pinpointing the exact action shows that you're taking responsibility for your behavior, not just the unfortunate outcome.

Let's take a common example: you yelled at your partner. "I'm sorry I yelled at you" doesn't cut it. But saying, "I'm sorry I yelled at you because I was stressed from work, hadn't eaten all day cause I'm trying that stupid new intermittent fasting thing that I'm convinced was invented as a low-key torture tactic, and lost my temper" gives context and shows you understand the triggers behind your actions. It's a recognition that your actions weren't just random outbursts; they were influenced by specific factors that you can address and improve. By the way, if you can relate to the statement above, I feel you and take it easy on yourself - go have a bagel.

Acknowledging what you did to cause the damage also paves the way for better self-awareness and growth. If you realize that your hangry tendencies are a recurring issue, you can take steps to manage them. Maybe carry a snack in your bag, plan meals better, or practice mindfulness techniques to keep your mood in check. Also, if you do, by some miracle, figure out how to use mindfulness to push away food cravings please email me as I'm dying to figure that one out myself.

The necessity of clear and specific language in recognizing faults can't be overstated. While I don't suggest listing out everything you did wrong and then reading it like a shopping list of sins (you'll see in future chapters how you have to do some listening before any apologizing is done), it's important that you get clear on what you did. And I mean crystal clear, like the kind of clarity you get from staring at your reflection in a freshly cleaned window and realizing you've got spinach in your teeth.

Think about everything that led up to that moment. Replay the scene in your head like a movie, except this time you're the director who has to point out all the bloopers. Find that pivotal moment where you let your animal instincts take over and lead you down the path of wrong decisions. Was it when you decided to skip breakfast and turned into a hangry beast by noon? Was it when you chose to respond to that work email while driving, convincing yourself that multitasking was a brilliant idea? Multitasking - what a myth!

## Who Benefits From This First Step

Remember, there are really three entities that benefit from this first step of recognition: your partner, your relationship (and yes, that is its own thing), and you.

First, let's talk about your partner. When you take the time to recognize and articulate exactly what you did wrong, it shows your partner that you're not just paying lip service to the apology. You've put in the effort to understand their perspective and acknowledge the impact of your actions. This kind of sincere recognition can help mend hurt feelings and rebuild trust. It's like giving them a heartfelt "I'm sorry" wrapped in the shiny paper of self-awareness and tied with a bow of empathy.

Next, your relationship itself stands to benefit. Think of your relationship as a separate entity, like a house you both live in. Every time you recognize and address your faults, you're doing a bit of maintenance on that house. Maybe you're fixing a leaky roof or patching up a crack in the foundation. By being clear and specific in your apologies, you're strengthening the structure of your relationship, making it more resilient against future storms.

And let's not forget about you. Yes, you! The more you figure out where you went wrong, the more you can grow as a person. It's like leveling up in a video game, but instead of gaining extra lives or magical powers, you're gaining self-awareness and emotional intelligence. This growth isn't just beneficial for your current relationship; it's something you carry with you into all aspects of your life. You become better equipped to handle conflicts, make amends, and build stronger connections with others.

So, while the first step of recognition might feel a bit like ripping off a Band-Aid, remember that the benefits are threefold. Your partner feels heard and valued, your relationship becomes stronger and more resilient, and you grow into a more self-aware, emotionally intelligent individual. It's a win-win-win situation, and all it takes is a bit of honesty and introspection.

And hey, if you can master this step, you're well on your way to becoming an apology ninja, ready to tackle even the toughest of conflicts with grace and sincerity.

## Lack of Recognition in the Media

When someone fails to recognize what they did wrong with enough clarity and specificity, it feels like a forced apology and loses its potency. Instead of mending bridges, it leaves everyone involved wondering if they should start building a moat instead. Want an example? Of course you do—let's take a look at one where Pepsi wished it could retrace its steps:

# Apology Hall of Shame: Pepsi/Kendall Jenner 2017

In April 2017, Pepsi released an advertisement featuring Kendall Jenner that was intended to promote the brand as a unifying force during protests. The ad depicted Jenner joining a protest and ultimately handing a police officer a can of Pepsi, which seemingly resolved the tension between the protesters and the police. The message was clear: world peace could be achieved with a refreshing sip of soda. Who knew that the answer to racial tension in America was hiding inside the aluminum can of America's second largest cola brand? Maybe the cure for the Israel-Palestine conflict has been hiding inside a double-stuffed Oreo.

Naturally, this brilliant marketing move was met with widespread criticism for its insensitivity and trivialization of serious social justice movements, including Black Lives Matter.

The backlash was swift and fierce. People were not buying the idea that centuries of social struggle could be smoothed over with a can of cold pop and a Kardashian sister. The internet exploded with memes, parodies, and a general sense of "What were they thinking?"

Pepsi quickly realized they had stepped in it and tried to issue an apology. However, instead of acknowledging the specific ways the ad had missed the mark, Pepsi's initial response was more of a vague, corporate "whoopsie" than a heartfelt mea culpa.

Pepsi's initial apology read:

"Pepsi was trying to project a global message of unity, peace, and understanding. Clearly, we missed the mark, and we apologize. We did not intend to make light of any serious issue. We are removing the content and halting any further rollout. We also apologize for putting Kendall Jenner in this position."

So, why did Pepsi's apology crash and burn faster than a can of soda dropped from a skyscraper? Let's break it down:

## Lack of Recognition of the Specific Wrongdoing

Pepsi's apology focused on the intention behind the ad rather than acknowledging the specific reasons why it was offensive. It's like trying to explain to your partner that you meant well when you bought them a vacuum cleaner for their birthday. Intentions are nice and all, but if you don't recognize the actual problem—trivializing and co-opting significant social justice movements for commercial gain—you're just spinning your wheels. Pepsi needed to say, "We messed up by making light of serious issues," but instead they went with, "We meant well." Not the same thing, Pepsi. Not the same thing at all.

## Vague Language

By saying, "we missed the mark," Pepsi didn't explicitly state what the mark was or how they had missed it. This vagueness made the apology seem insincere and evasive. It's like telling someone, "I'm sorry for that thing I did." What thing? When? How? Details matter! If you're not clear about what you did wrong, people are left guessing, and that's never a good look. Pepsi needed to be specific: "We missed the mark by turning a serious protest into a soda commercial."

## Deflection

By mentioning Kendall Jenner and apologizing for putting her in a difficult position, Pepsi seemed to shift some of the focus away from their own responsibility in creating and approving the ad. Also, personally it makes me think that some of Kendall Jenner's team got pissed about the negative social media reaction and pushed Pepsi to say sorry and try to make things right - but it just blew up in their face.

What Pepsi did is like apologizing for a bad gift by saying, "I'm sorry you didn't like it, and I'm also sorry that the store was out of better options." By dragging Kendall Jenner into the mix, Pepsi came off like they were trying to deflect some of the blame and pacify Kendall Jenner's publicists - and they did neither.

## Lack of Empathy

The apology did not convey genuine empathy for the people who were hurt or offended by the ad. It was more about damage control than making amends. It's the difference between saying, "I'm sorry you're upset" and "I'm sorry I hurt you." One is a platitude, the other is an actual acknowledgment of pain. Pepsi's apology felt like a corporate press release designed to stem the bleeding rather than a heartfelt attempt to make things right. They needed to show they understood the gravity of their misstep and genuinely cared about the impact it had.

## The Backlash

The backlash against Pepsi and Kendall Jenner was swift and intense. Social media erupted with criticism faster than you can say "Pepsi challenge." Memes, tweets, and think-pieces flooded the internet, all highlighting just how out of touch Pepsi seemed with the real issues faced by activists. It was as if Pepsi had tried to put out a fire with gasoline—only in this case, the gasoline was a fizzy soft drink.

The ad was quickly pulled, but the damage to Pepsi's reputation lingered like the aftertaste of a flat soda. The company became the poster child for what not to do in a public relations crisis. People weren't just upset; they were pointing and laughing. Pepsi's attempt at damage control was akin to trying to plug a volcano with a cork—it didn't go well.

In response to the ongoing criticism, Pepsi had to put in some serious elbow grease to rebuild trust with its audience. They emphasized a more thoughtful approach to future marketing campaigns, promising to listen and learn from their mistakes. This involved consulting with real activists and ensuring their future messages didn't come off as tone-deaf stunts.

The incident serves as a reminder of the importance of understanding and respecting the cultural and social contexts in which advertising content is released. It's a lesson in the pitfalls of good intentions executed poorly and the critical need for companies to be genuinely aware of the issues they're addressing.

## What Could They Have Done Differently?

You might be tempted to say that Pepsi should have just not made the commercial in the first place. And, sure, that's a solid strategy for avoiding a PR nightmare. But that kind of gets away from the purpose of this book. We're operating on the assumption that people, companies, countries, and communities are going to make mistakes—big, juicy, facepalm-inducing mistakes. And when they do, the art of a proper apology comes into play.

So, with that knowledge in hand, let's take a look at how an apology that truly recognizes Pepsi's role in the matter might have sounded:

*Pepsi sincerely apologizes for the recent advertisement featuring Kendall Jenner. We understand and recognize that the ad trivialized important social justice movements, including Black Lives Matter, by co-opting their imagery and message for commercial purposes. This was a mistake, and we deeply regret the insensitivity and offense it has caused.*

*We acknowledge that our attempt to promote unity and peace was misguided and failed to reflect the serious nature of the issues being protested. The ad undermined the real struggles and experiences of people fighting for justice and equality.*

*We take full responsibility for this error in judgment and are committed to learning from this experience. Moving forward, we will work closely with advocacy groups, activists, and communities to ensure that our marketing efforts respect and accurately represent their voices and causes.*

*We apologize to the activists who are working tirelessly for social justice and to our customers who were hurt or offended by the ad. We promise to do better and to be more thoughtful and respectful in our future endeavors.*

*Thank you for holding us accountable.*

The one thing I haven't been able to figure out though is how to get all of that to fit on a tweet - or whatever the heck X is calling it now.

# ENJOYING THE BOOK? PLEASE CONSIDER WRITING A REVIEW ON AMAZON

As a small independent publisher, one of the absolute best ways you can support our work is by leaving us a review on Amazon to let people know your honest thoughts about this book.

1. Open the camera on your phone
2. Point the camera at the QR code above
3. Open the link and write an honest review
4. Enjoy our gratitude for your help

# 6

# The Guilt Roller Coaster: Surviving Remorse

LET'S KICK THINGS OFF with a deep dive into what remorse actually is. Spoiler alert: it's not just feeling bad because you got caught.

Think back to a time when you really messed up. Maybe you accidentally spilled coffee on your boss's laptop or forgot your partner's birthday (again). That sinking feeling in your stomach? That's not quite remorse. That's more like panic mixed with a dash of regret.

Remorse is different. It's a profound, often uncomfortable, recognition that you've done something wrong and it's caused harm to someone else. It's not just about you and your guilt trip—it's about truly understanding the impact of your actions on another person. It's a little bit like getting hit by a truckload of empathy.

Let's break it down further. Regret is usually self-focused. You might regret missing out on a party or not studying for a test. Remorse, on the other hand, is other-focused. It's about realizing you've hurt someone and feeling a deep, genuine sorrow for their suffering.

Imagine you borrowed your friend's car and, in a moment of distraction, scratched it against a fence. Regret is feeling bad because now you have to pay for the damage and endure your friend's wrath. Remorse is feeling terrible because you know your friend trusted you with their car, and you betrayed that trust. See the difference?

Feeling remorse is like having a built-in moral compass. It's your inner voice telling you that you've veered off course. It's what makes us human. Without remorse, we'd be like robots programmed to go through the motions without ever really connecting with the people around us.

And here's the kicker: feeling remorse is crucial for a genuine apology. If you don't feel that deep sense of regret for the pain you've caused, your apology will come off as hollow. It's like trying to bake a cake without flour—it just doesn't work.

## A Quick Thought Experiment

Imagine having a superpower that lets you relive any moment in your life, but with a twist—you get to experience it from the other person's perspective. Sounds like something out of a sci-fi movie, right? But stay with me here.

Let's say you're a salesperson. You've got your pitch down to a science, but imagine if you could step into your customer's shoes. You'd feel their excitement, their hesitation, maybe even their frustration as you try to upsell them on something they don't really need. Suddenly, that "killer pitch" feels a bit more like a pushy sales tactic.

Now, let's take it up a notch. Imagine being able to relive that mean remark you made to your mother, but this time, as your mother. You're no longer the one dishing out the snide comment; you're the one receiving it. You feel the sting, the disappointment, maybe even the confusion as to why your beloved child would say something so hurtful. Ouch, right?

This little mental exercise is what remorse is all about. It's about stepping out of your own shoes and into someone else's. It's about feeling their hurt, understanding their perspective, and realizing the impact of your actions on them.

Think about the last time you had a heated argument with your partner. You might have been so wrapped up in your own feelings—anger, frustration, the need to be right—that you didn't stop to think about how they were feeling. But if you could hit rewind and view the argument through their eyes, you might see things differently. You'd feel their sadness, their sense of betrayal, their longing for understanding. That's remorse knocking on your heart's door, asking you to recognize the real impact of your words and actions.

This perspective shift isn't just about feeling guilty; it's about developing empathy. It's what makes an apology genuine. When you truly understand how your actions have affected someone else, your remorse becomes the foundation for a heartfelt apology. It's no longer just about saying "I'm sorry"; it's about showing that you've walked a mile in their shoes and you genuinely regret the hurt you've caused.

### How Does It Make You Feel, Though?

Alright, so you've put yourself in the other person's shoes, and you're starting to feel the weight of what you did. But what exactly are you feeling? Let's take a ride on the emotional roller coaster that is genuine remorse.

### The Guilt Trip

First stop: guilt. This is usually the first emotion to rear its head. It's that nagging feeling in the pit of your stomach that whispers, "You really messed up this time." Guilt is your conscience's way of reminding you that you've strayed off the moral path. It's uncomfortable, sure, but it's also a sign that you care about the impact of your actions.

## Shame, Shame, Shame

Next up is shame. If guilt is the whisper, shame is the full-blown shout. It's not just about what you did; it's about who you are. Shame makes you feel like you're a bad person because of your actions. It's a heavier, more personal feeling that can be tough to shake. But here's the thing: while shame can be paralyzing, it can also be a powerful motivator for change if you channel it correctly.

## Empathy Overload

Now, let's talk about empathy. When you truly feel remorse, you're flooded with empathy for the person you've hurt. This isn't just a fleeting "Oh, that must have sucked for them" kind of feeling. It's a deep, visceral understanding of their pain. You're feeling their sadness, their disappointment, their anger. It's like your heart is breaking right alongside theirs.

## Regret: The Sibling of Remorse

Regret is closely related to remorse, but it's worth mentioning separately. Regret is that wish-you-could-turn-back-time feeling. It's the "If only I had…" thoughts that play on repeat in your mind. Regret can be productive, pushing you to think about what you could have done differently. But beware: too much regret can lead to wallowing, and that's not helpful for anyone.

## A Bit of Fear

Then there's fear. This might seem out of place, but when you feel genuine remorse, there's often a fear of the consequences. Fear of losing a relationship, fear of tarnishing your reputation, fear of not being forgiven. It's a natural part of the emotional mix, but it shouldn't overshadow the more constructive emotions like guilt and empathy.

## Sorrow: The Heart of Remorse

At the heart of it all is sorrow. This isn't just feeling bad; it's feeling deeply saddened by the hurt you've caused. Sorrow is what drives you to want to make things right. It's the emotional core of remorse that fuels the desire for genuine amends.

## A Glimmer of Hope

Finally, amidst all these heavy emotions, there's a glimmer of hope. Genuine remorse comes with the hope for redemption. The belief that, despite your mistake, you can make things better. This hope is what keeps you moving forward, striving to heal the hurt you've caused and to become a better person in the process. Cling to this hope when you find it because this is the easiest way to make amends and clear the path to a better future.

## The Roller coaster Ride

Feeling genuine remorse is like being on an emotional rollercoaster. You can experience guilt, shame, empathy, regret, fear, sorrow, and, ultimately, hope. You don't always feel all of them, but they're all there like a heartache buffet waiting for you to grab a plate and go. It's not an easy ride, but it's often a necessary one if you want to offer a sincere apology. Each emotion has its own role in helping you understand the depth of your mistake and the impact it's had on the other person.

Embrace these feelings. Let them guide you towards making things right. Remember, it's through this emotional journey that you'll find the strength to offer a heartfelt apology and start the healing process.

## The Psychological Necessity of Remorse

You might be wondering why feeling genuine remorse is more than just a moral obligation. Well, it's actually a cornerstone of personal growth. Let's start with the concept of emotional accountability.

## Owning Your Actions

Imagine you're a kid again, and you've just broken your neighbor's window with an ill-advised baseball throw. Your first instinct might be to hide or blame the kid next door, but deep down, you know you're responsible. Owning up to it means facing the music, admitting you were at fault, and doing something to fix it. That's emotional accountability in a nutshell.

In the grown-up world, it's much the same. When you mess up, taking responsibility for your actions is crucial. It means acknowledging that your actions have consequences and that you have a role in creating those consequences. This isn't about self-flagellation; it's about honesty and integrity.

## The Path to Personal Growth

Why is this so important for personal growth? Because without acknowledging your mistakes, you're doomed to repeat them. It's like driving with a blindfold on—you're going to keep crashing into things until you take it off and see where you're going wrong.

When you feel genuine remorse, you're taking the first step towards emotional accountability. You're saying, "Yes, I messed up, and I see how it affected you." This recognition is the seed from which personal growth sprouts.

## Learning and Evolving

Consider this: every mistake is a learning opportunity. When you take responsibility for your actions, you're opening yourself up to these lessons. You're looking at your behavior critically and thinking about how you can do better next time. It's like upgrading your internal software—you're constantly improving and evolving.

I once worked with a client, let's call her Susan, who had a habit of snapping at her coworkers. She didn't see it as a big deal until she noticed people avoiding her in the break room. Through our sessions, Susan began to understand the impact of her behavior. Feeling genuine remorse, she took responsibility and started working on her communication skills. Not only did her relationships at work improve, but she also grew as a person, becoming more patient and empathetic.

## Building Integrity and Trust

Taking responsibility also builds integrity and trust. When people see that you're willing to own up to your mistakes, they're more likely to trust you. It shows that you're reliable and honest, traits that are invaluable in any relationship, personal or professional.

Think about it: would you rather work with someone who always blames others for their mistakes or someone who admits when they've messed up and takes steps to make it right? The latter is someone you can trust, someone who you know will handle things responsibly.

## Breaking the Cycle

Emotional accountability breaks the cycle of blame and defensiveness. When you refuse to take responsibility, you're stuck in a loop of denial and justification. This doesn't just hurt others—it stunts your own growth. You're not learning, you're not evolving, and you're certainly not becoming a better version of yourself.

By contrast, when you feel genuine remorse and take responsibility, you're breaking free from this cycle. You're embracing your imperfections and using them as stepping stones to become a better person. It's not about being perfect; it's about being real and striving to improve.

## The Courage to Change

Ultimately, taking responsibility requires courage. It's not easy to admit when you're wrong or to face the consequences of your actions. But it's this courage that drives personal growth. It's what pushes you to learn from your mistakes, to make amends, and to become a better, more empathetic person.

## Internal Conflict

Now, let's explore the internal conflict that often accompanies genuine remorse. This is where cognitive dissonance comes into play.

## The Discomfort of Contradiction

Cognitive dissonance is that uncomfortable feeling you get when your actions don't align with your values or beliefs. It's like your brain is playing tug-of-war with itself. On one hand, you see yourself as a kind and considerate person; on the other, you've just done something that contradicts that image.

## The Role of Cognitive Dissonance

This internal conflict is crucial for fostering genuine remorse. When you experience cognitive dissonance, your mind is motivated to resolve the contradiction. This often leads to a moment of reckoning where you confront your actions and their impact. It's in this moment of discomfort that genuine remorse can take root.

**Embracing the Discomfort**

Feeling cognitive dissonance isn't pleasant, but it's a sign that your moral compass is working. Embrace the discomfort—it's your mind's way of nudging you towards better behavior. By resolving this internal conflict, you're not just alleviating your own discomfort; you're also taking a step towards making amends and improving your relationships.

**Moral Compass**

Let's talk about how remorse aligns with our innate sense of right and wrong. We all have an internal moral compass that guides our actions and decisions.

**Tuning into Your Moral Compass**

When you feel genuine remorse, it's like your moral compass is pointing due north. It's telling you that you've strayed off course and it's time to correct your path. This internal guidance system is what helps us distinguish right from wrong, and remorse is a key indicator that we've veered into the wrong territory.

**Reinforcing Ethical Behavior**

Feeling remorse reinforces ethical behavior. It's a signal that you value integrity and want to uphold it in your interactions. By acknowledging your mistakes and feeling sorry for them, you're realigning yourself with your core values. This not only helps you grow as a person but also fosters trust and respect in your relationships.

**Moral Growth and Development**

Our moral compass isn't fixed; it develops and refines over time through experiences and reflections. When you feel remorse, you're engaging in moral growth.

You're learning from your mistakes, understanding their impact, and making a conscious effort to do better. This ongoing process is what shapes you into a more empathetic, responsible, and morally grounded individual.

## Practical Strategies to Cultivate Remorse

Time to get down to the nitty-gritty of how to actually cultivate remorse. Because, let's face it, sometimes it's hard to feel genuinely sorry when you're busy juggling life's chaos. Here's where mindfulness practices come in, helping you become more aware of the impact of your actions without having to sign up for a year-long meditation retreat.

## Mindfulness: The Power of Pausing

First up, let's talk about the power of pausing. Imagine you're in a heated argument with your partner about whose turn it is to take out the trash. You're about to unleash a zinger, but instead, you hit the pause button. This magical pause gives you a moment to breathe, reflect, and consider the impact of your words.

Think of it as the superhero ability to stop time, minus the spandex suit. By taking a brief moment to pause, you can avoid saying something you'll regret and start feeling that twinge of remorse before you've even messed up. It's like having a pre-emptive guilt trip, but in a good way.

## The Body Scan Technique

Next, let's dive into the body scan technique. No, this isn't some sci-fi device. It's a mindfulness practice where you mentally scan your body from head to toe, checking in on how you feel. This helps you become more aware of physical sensations linked to emotions. Are your shoulders tense? Is your jaw clenched? These could be signs that you're about to do or say something regrettable.

By tuning into your body, you can catch these red flags early. It's like having an internal warning system that says, "Danger! Danger! You're about to step on a metaphorical landmine!" A quick body scan can help you slow down and reflect on the potential impact of your actions, steering you towards remorse and away from trouble.

### The Daily Reflection Ritual

Now, let's get a bit more traditional with the daily reflection ritual. Every evening, take a few minutes to sit quietly and reflect on your day. Ask yourself questions like, "Did I hurt anyone's feelings today?" or "Did I act in a way that I'm not proud of?" This isn't about beating yourself up; it's about honest self-assessment.

Think of it as a mini therapy session with yourself. You're holding up a mirror to your actions and examining them with a critical but kind eye. Over time, this practice helps you become more attuned to the impact of your behavior, making it easier to feel genuine remorse when you've slipped up.

### The Gratitude Journal with a Twist

Lastly, consider keeping a gratitude journal with a twist. Each day, write down something you're grateful for and one thing you wish you'd handled differently. This practice keeps you grounded in positivity while also encouraging self-improvement. It's a balanced approach that fosters a healthy sense of remorse without dragging you into a pit of despair.

By integrating these mindfulness practices into your daily routine, you'll become more aware of the impact of your actions and more adept at feeling genuine remorse. It's like giving your conscience a daily workout, ensuring it stays in tip-top shape. So, take a pause, scan your body, reflect on your day, practice empathy, and jot down your thoughts. Your relationships—and your own sense of integrity—will thank you for it.

### Seeking Feedback: How Input from Others Can Help You Recognize the Need for Remorse

If mindfulness practices are like personal trainers for your conscience, seeking feedback is like hiring a coach who's not afraid to tell you when you're missing the mark. It's not always comfortable, but it's incredibly effective.

### The Courage to Ask

First things first: asking for feedback takes guts. It's like voluntarily signing up for a critique session of your life's choices. But here's the thing—it's also one of the most direct routes to recognizing where you've gone wrong. When you open yourself up to feedback, you're essentially saying, "I want to be better, and I need your help to get there."

### The Honest Mirror

When you seek feedback, you're looking into an honest mirror held up by someone else. This mirror doesn't have any of the flattering lighting or Instagram filters you might use to soften the edges. It shows you the raw, unedited version of your actions and their impact.

Let's say you're at work, and you've just finished a big project. You think you nailed it, but there's a nagging feeling that maybe, just maybe, not everyone is as thrilled as you are. Instead of basking in the glow of your own perceived brilliance, you decide to ask your team for their thoughts. Brace yourself, because here comes the honesty train.

### The Gift of Perspective

Getting feedback from others gives you a fresh perspective. Sometimes, we're so close to our own actions that we can't see their full impact. It's like trying to read a book with your nose pressed against the pages. You need someone to pull you back and give you the bigger picture.

For example, you might think your sarcastic comments at the dinner table are just harmless jokes. But when you ask your family for feedback, you might learn that those "jokes" are actually hurtful and make others feel belittled. Ouch. It's a tough pill to swallow, but it's crucial for fostering genuine remorse.

### The Importance of a Safe Space

Now, let's be clear: not all feedback is created equal. It's important to seek input from people you trust—those who have your best interests at heart and who can provide constructive criticism without tearing you down. Creating a safe space for feedback ensures that you're getting insights that are both honest and helpful.

Imagine you've been feeling a bit distant from your best friend lately. Instead of letting the relationship drift, you muster up the courage to ask, "Hey, have I done something to upset you?" This opens the door for them to share their perspective and for you to understand the impact of your actions.

### Applying the Feedback

Finally, feedback is only valuable if you do something with it. It's like getting a map to hidden treasure and then using it as a coaster for your coffee cup. Take the insights you've gained and apply them to your behavior. Make a conscious effort to change and improve.

If you've learned that your constant interruptions during meetings are frustrating your colleagues, make a deliberate effort to listen more and speak less. By acting on the feedback, you're not only showing that you value their input, but you're also demonstrating a genuine desire to grow and improve.

## Embracing Growth

Seeking feedback is a powerful tool for cultivating remorse. It helps you see the blind spots you might have missed on your own. It's not always easy to hear, but it's essential for personal growth and building stronger, more empathetic relationships.

So, don't be afraid to ask for feedback. Embrace the honest mirror, listen actively, and apply what you've learned. It's through this process that you'll become more aware of the impact of your actions and better equipped to feel and express genuine remorse. And who knows? You might even find that the treasure map leads to a better version of yourself, one feedback session at a time.

## Therapeutic Techniques: Professional Methods to Access and Process Feelings of Remorse

If you're not super DIY about the remorse button and need some professional guidance, I got your back. Let's dive into the world of therapeutic techniques—those magical tools that professionals use to help you access and process feelings of remorse. These methods are like the Swiss Army knives of emotional healing, packed with nifty features to help you navigate your way through the dense forest of guilt and regret.

### Cognitive Behavioral Therapy (CBT)

First up, we have Cognitive Behavioral Therapy, or CBT for short. Think of CBT as a mental workout that helps you reshape your thought patterns. It's like taking your brain to the gym, but without the sweaty gym clothes.

CBT focuses on identifying and challenging negative thoughts and beliefs. When it comes to remorse, CBT can help you break down those overwhelming feelings into manageable chunks. By examining your thoughts and behaviors, you can understand the root cause of your remorse and develop healthier ways to cope with and learn from your mistakes.

## The Empty Chair Technique

Next, let's talk about the empty chair technique. This one's a bit of a classic in the therapy world. Imagine you're in a room with an empty chair. Now, picture the person you've wronged sitting in that chair. Yep, it's like a scene from an emotional drama, but without the dramatic lighting and background music.

In this exercise, you speak to the empty chair as if the person you've hurt is sitting right there. You express your feelings, apologize, and even listen to what you imagine their response might be. It's a powerful way to externalize your remorse and gain insight into the other person's perspective. Plus, it's a safe space to practice your apology without the fear of immediate repercussions.

## Narrative Therapy

Don't forget about narrative therapy. This approach helps you reframe your personal story, viewing your life as a series of interconnected narratives. Think of it as editing your own movie, where you get to change the script and add some uplifting plot twists.

In narrative therapy, you explore the stories you tell yourself about your actions and their impact. By examining and re-authoring these narratives, you can gain a new perspective on your mistakes and how they fit into the broader context of your life. This technique helps you see remorse not as a burden, but as a chapter in your journey towards growth and self-improvement.

## Emotion-Focused Therapy (EFT)

Emotion-Focused Therapy (EFT) is another fantastic tool. EFT emphasizes the importance of emotions in personal development and healing. It's like having a guided tour through your emotional landscape, helping you navigate the tricky terrain of remorse.

With EFT, you work on identifying, experiencing, and processing your emotions in a supportive environment. This approach allows you to delve deep into your feelings of remorse, understanding their origins and significance. By fully experiencing these emotions, you can move towards genuine healing and transformation.

## Guided Imagery

Lastly, let's explore guided imagery. This technique involves using vivid mental images to explore your feelings and gain insight into your experiences. It's like taking a mental vacation, but instead of lounging on a beach, you're diving into the depths of your psyche.

A therapist might guide you through a visualization where you imagine a situation where you felt remorse. You explore the scene, the emotions, and the consequences in detail. This immersive experience can help you process your remorse more deeply and find new ways to make amends and move forward.

## Embracing Professional Help

These therapeutic techniques are powerful tools for accessing and processing feelings of remorse. They provide structured and supportive ways to explore your emotions, understand their impact, and use them as catalysts for personal growth. If you find yourself struggling with remorse, don't hesitate to seek out a professional who can guide you through these methods. It's like having a seasoned sherpa lead you up the mountain of emotional healing.

# Apology Hall of Shame: Facebook and the Cambridge Analytica Data Breach 2018

Alright, folks, buckle up because we're about to dive into a masterclass on what not to do when it comes to expressing remorse. We're looking at none other than Facebook's infamous handling of the Cambridge Analytica data breach. If you ever wanted to see how not showing remorse can backfire spectacularly, this is the case study for you.

### The Incident: What Happened?

In 2018, the world was rocked by the revelation that Cambridge Analytica, a British political consulting firm, had harvested the personal data of millions of Facebook users without their consent. This data was then used to influence political campaigns, including the 2016 U.S. presidential election. The breach exposed the dark underbelly of data privacy and left countless users feeling violated and manipulated.

Here's the lowdown: Cambridge Analytica created a seemingly innocuous personality quiz app. When users took the quiz, they unknowingly granted access not only to their own data but also to the data of their Facebook friends. This allowed Cambridge Analytica to compile a massive dataset on millions of unsuspecting users. The information was then used to create highly targeted political ads, exploiting personal details to sway voters' opinions and behavior.

The fallout was immense. Users felt betrayed, trust in Facebook plummeted, and the company faced intense scrutiny from regulators, politicians, and the public worldwide. The breach highlighted serious flaws in Facebook's data security and raised critical questions about user privacy and the ethical use of personal information.

## The Lack of Remorse: How Facebook Fumbled the Response

Now, let's talk about Facebook's response—or lack thereof. When the scandal broke, Mark Zuckerberg, the face of Facebook, was summoned to testify before Congress. If you've seen any clips from that hearing, you might remember Zuckerberg looking about as remorseful as a robot caught sneaking a midnight oil change.

Instead of heartfelt apologies and genuine remorse, Zuckerberg's testimony was filled with robotic, rehearsed responses. He appeared detached, more concerned with legal jargon and damage control than with the actual pain and suffering caused to millions of users. His demeanor was stiff, his responses carefully scripted, and any semblance of genuine regret was noticeably absent.

Let's break down the key moments that showcased Facebook's complete lack of remorse:

1. The Non-Apology Apology: Zuckerberg's statements were filled with classic non-apology phrases like, "We made mistakes," and "We need to do better." These are the corporate equivalents of saying, "Sorry if you were offended," without actually acknowledging any wrongdoing.

2. Deflection and Denial: Instead of taking full responsibility, Facebook's leadership often deflected blame, pointing fingers at Cambridge Analytica and third-party developers. This move not only failed to address the core issue but also came off as evasive and insincere.

3. Lack of Empathy: Throughout the hearings and subsequent public statements, there was a noticeable absence of empathy. Zuckerberg's robotic delivery and lack of emotional connection made it seem like he was reading off a script rather than genuinely engaging with the gravity of the situation.

4. Business as Usual: Despite the massive breach of trust, Facebook's approach was largely business as usual. There were no immediate,

sweeping changes to reassure users that their data would be protected moving forward. Instead, the company's actions suggested that it was more focused on weathering the storm than on making meaningful changes.

5. Public Backlash: The lack of genuine remorse didn't go unnoticed. Users, privacy advocates, and politicians criticized Facebook for its tepid response. The company's stock took a hit, and its reputation suffered long-lasting damage.

**The Fallout: Lessons in Remorse**

The Facebook-Cambridge Analytica scandal serves as a cautionary tale about the importance of showing genuine remorse. When a company fails to acknowledge the impact of its actions and express sincere regret, it loses trust and credibility. Facebook's mishandling of the situation not only damaged its relationship with users but also highlighted the need for greater transparency and accountability in the tech industry.

**The Missed Opportunity: How Mark Zuckerberg Could Have Easily Expressed Remorse**

Alright, let's talk about how Mark Zuckerberg could have turned this entire fiasco around with a few simple, heartfelt words. It's not rocket science, folks—just basic human empathy and accountability. Imagine if, instead of coming off as a robotic CEO, Zuckerberg had shown a shred of genuine remorse. The public's reaction could have been entirely different.

**The Simplicity of Genuine Remorse**

Expressing genuine remorse isn't about delivering a flawless speech or performing a dramatic mea culpa. It's about being real, honest, and human. Zuckerberg could have acknowledged the impact, taken full responsibility (something rarely seen done by CEOs), shown empathy, and laid out concrete steps to rectify the situation.

Now, picture this: Zuckerberg at the congressional hearing, not as the stiff, rehearsed executive we saw, but as a CEO genuinely committed to making things right. Here's what he could have said:

*"Chairman, members of the committee, and everyone watching today, I want to begin by saying I am deeply sorry for the role Facebook played in the Cambridge Analytica data breach. I understand that this incident has caused significant distress, anger, and a loss of trust among our users, and I take full responsibility for what happened.*

*When people entrust us with their personal information, they have every right to expect that it will be protected. We failed to meet those expectations, and for that, I am profoundly sorry.*

*I want to acknowledge the real-world impact this has had on millions of people. Many of you feel violated and betrayed. Your personal data was misused in ways you did not consent to, and that is unacceptable. I understand that our actions—or lack thereof—have caused real harm, and I am here to take full responsibility for that.*

*We need to do better. And we will. Moving forward, Facebook is committed to implementing stringent data protection measures to ensure that this never happens again. We are overhauling our data privacy policies, increasing transparency, and enhancing our security protocols. Additionally, we will be conducting a thorough audit of all third-party applications to ensure compliance with our updated standards.*

*But beyond these technical changes, I want to assure you that we are fostering a culture of accountability and empathy within our company. We are listening to your feedback, learning from our mistakes, and making the necessary changes to regain your trust.*

*Thank you for holding us accountable. We are committed to earning back your trust through our actions and ongoing commitment to protecting your privacy."*

## The Impact of a Sincere Apology

Had Zuckerberg delivered a statement like this, it would have demonstrated genuine remorse and a commitment to change. It's a stark contrast to the impersonal, robotic responses we saw. This approach could have gone a long way in mending the relationship between Facebook and its users, showing that the company truly cares about their well-being. Just to be clear, I think the members of congress who chastised him probably would have still done so and insisted that he pay everyone personally for damages caused which is just not realistic but at least he would have had a chance to win some people over who were watching.

# 7

# Are They Ready Yet? Apology Timing 101

LET'S GET ONE THING straight: timing an apology is everything. It's like trying to deliver a punchline—do it too soon, and you're met with blank stares; too late, and the moment's gone. Now, imagine that punchline is actually you groveling for forgiveness. Yeah, the stakes are a bit higher.

An apology can sometimes do more harm than good if not timed properly. Picture this: you've just stepped on a landmine, and instead of waiting for the dust to settle, you rush in with a quick "sorry." Not the brightest idea, right? The fallout can be brutal. Instead of diffusing the situation, you might end up escalating it, making things worse for both of you.

Understanding when your partner is ready to hear an apology is crucial. You wouldn't try to explain quantum physics to someone having a meltdown, so why attempt an apology when emotions are running high? Look for signs that your partner might not be ready—visible anger, emotional distress, or complete withdrawal. These are your cues to hit pause and hold off on your apology.

Checking if your partner is ready to hear you out isn't just a nice-to-have—it's a game-changer. It prevents further conflict and shows you actually respect their feelings. It's like saying, "Hey, I messed up, and I want to make it right, but only when you're ready." It's a small gesture that can make a massive difference in how your apology is received.

So, before you dive headfirst into apology mode, take a beat. Ask yourself, "Is now really the right time?" If you're unsure, it's better to wait. Trust me, a well-timed apology is way more effective than a rushed, half-baked one.

## Understanding Readiness

So, what does it mean for your partner to be "ready" to hear an apology? It's not as simple as waiting for the steam to stop coming out of their ears—though that's a good start. Readiness means your partner is in a place where they can actually hear and process what you're saying without wanting to strangle you.

## Signs Your Partner Might Not Be Ready

First off, let's talk about the red flags that scream "now is not the time." If your partner looks like they could audition for the role of Angry Hulk, chances are they're not ready. Visible anger, like clenched fists or a furrowed brow, is a pretty solid indicator that you should hold off. Emotional distress is another biggie—if they're crying or look deeply hurt, pushing for an apology can backfire spectacularly. And then there's withdrawal: if your partner is giving you the silent treatment or has retreated to their "I need space" zone, respect it. Trying to apologize now is like trying to defuse a bomb with a sledgehammer.

## Benefits of Checking for Readiness

Why bother checking if they're ready, you ask? Well, checking for readiness can prevent further conflict. It shows you're not just trying to tick the "apology" box and move on, but that you genuinely care about their emotional state. This approach fosters mutual respect and can pave the way for a more effective, heartfelt apology.

Imagine this: instead of launching into a half-baked "sorry" while your partner is still fuming, you wait. You ask, "Is this a good time to talk about what happened?" This simple question can be a game-changer. It shows you're considerate of their feelings and can significantly lower the tension. If your partner says they're ready to hear an apology, you're already halfway to forgiveness. It means they're open to listening and potentially resolving the issue, which is a huge step forward.

Understanding and respecting your partner's readiness isn't just a nice gesture—it's essential. It's the difference between throwing a bucket of water on a grease fire versus letting it cool down before cleaning up the mess. So, next time you're gearing up to apologize, take a moment to assess the situation. Is your partner ready to hear you out, or are they still in the "I might murder you" phase?

## How to Ask if Your Partner is Ready

Figuring out the time is wrong is something you should be able to do by observation alone, but knowing if the timing is right is something you should always ask. There's multiple reasons for it, which we'll get to in a moment, but for now let's talk about how to ask if your partner is ready to hear your apology. You don't want to blurt it out awkwardly or come off as insincere. Here's how to approach it with finesse.

## Phrasing the Question: Suggestions on How to Ask

The key here is to be gentle and considerate. You want to show that you genuinely care about their emotional state. Here are some ways to phrase the question:

- "I want to apologize for what happened. Are you ready to talk about it now, or should we find a better time?"

- "I would like to say sorry for what I said earlier. Are you open to hearing an apology right now?

- "Would it be possible for me to apologize for that dumb thing I did to you now or are you too upset to hear that right now?"

You'll notice that all these approaches share the same essential core components. They signal that you're ready to apologize—because just saying "sorry" went out the window once you graduated from pull-ups. Sure, you could've tossed out a quick "sorry," but no, you're here to deliver a prime apology, the kind you'd want to record and stick on the refrigerator for everyone to admire.

Another thing these statements have in common is your willingness to wait until your partner is ready. Why is this important? It does two really useful things, especially if your relationship is on the rocks. First, it shows you're mindful of your partner's feelings—something they might not be feeling if you've messed up. You might already be on their bad list, so this alone can be a refreshing change of pace.

Second, it forces your partner to consider whether they're ready to hear an apology. When we're angry, we don't usually focus on what we need to calm down from that anger shelf we perch ourselves on. And that shelf is a nasty place, where things can be forgotten—like that top shelf in your pantry where you occasionally find ten-year-old brownie mix that could now power a small reactor.

When you ask if they're ready to hear an apology, they have to check in with themselves. If the answer is yes, that means they've already softened. They might not even realize they were ready until you asked, but the moment you muster up the courage to ask, a series of neurons fire off in their brain like a starting gun at a race. Within a second or two, they figure out if they're ready or not.

Before we even get to the actual apology, let's talk about how to ask your partner if they're ready to hear it. This step is crucial. Remember, we're not even apologizing yet; we're just setting the table here. The wrong words can derail the whole process before it even begins. So, let's dive into what not to say when you're trying to get your partner ready to hear your apology.

**"Can we just get this over with?"**

This screams impatience and dismissiveness. It's like telling them their feelings are a chore you want to check off your to-do list. Not exactly the vibe you want to set.

**"Are you finally ready to hear me out?"**

Using "finally" implies they've been dragging their feet or being unreasonable. It subtly shifts the blame onto them for not being ready sooner, which can make them defensive.

**"I don't have all day. Are you ready to listen?"**

Time constraints are the enemy of a good apology. This phrase suggests that your schedule is more important than their feelings, which can make them feel undervalued.

**"You can't still be mad, right?"**

This minimizes their emotions and suggests that their anger has an expiration date. It's a surefire way to make them feel like their feelings are invalid or overblown.

**"Let's just get this out of the way."**

Treating the apology process like an unpleasant task to be rushed through shows a lack of genuine concern. It's like saying, "Let's hurry up and deal with your irrational feelings so we can move on."

Using any of these phrases is like trying to start a race by tripping over the starting line. You want to create a space where your partner feels heard and respected, not rushed or ridiculed. Choose your words with care, show that you genuinely want to make things right, and avoid any hint of impatience or condescension. The goal is to set a positive tone for the apology that follows, paving the way for genuine reconciliation.

## Tone and Body Language: Unsung Heroes of Apologizing

Just as important and sometimes even more important than the words you choose to use when asking if your partner is ready to hear an apology are the tone and body language you project. First let's talk about your tone because a lot of people get this one dead wrong.

Imagine you've just sideswiped a cop car, and that car is now wrapped around a tree. The temptation to pull a Houdini and vanish is strong, but your moral compass kicks in. You have to check on the officer. As you approach the car, heart pounding, you see the cop is conscious but bleeding. You move cautiously and, with a voice that's soft and shaky, you ask, "Are you okay?" That's the tone you need when asking your partner if they're ready to hear an apology. This isn't the time for bravado or nonchalance; it's about genuine concern and vulnerability.

## The Power of Body Language

Body language can make or break your apology attempt before you've even started speaking. Picture this: you're getting ready to apologize, but your body's in fight-or-flight mode. Your head leans back, your arms are up defensively—it's like you're about to go twelve rounds in a boxing ring. Your partner, whether they realize it or not, picks up on this and mirrors your defensiveness.

Instead, you want to channel your inner humble pie. Lean forward slightly, head tilted in, eyes sad and concerned. Practice in the mirror if you need to—it's worth the awkwardness. Think of it as a down payment on avoiding those sky-high divorce attorney fees. Spend ten minutes perfecting your "I'm genuinely sorry" face, and you might save yourself from years of regret.

## Hands: The Great Communicators

Now, what do you do with your hands? Here's a pro tip: hold them up at chest height with your palms open. This non-threatening gesture says, "I come in peace." It's like when a medieval knight approaches a castle, hands empty to show they're not carrying a weapon. Your partner's defenses are up, scanning for any signs of a sneak attack. Showing your open palms can disarm them and make them more receptive.

In all seriousness, this works wonders. I use it in my counseling sessions all the time. When one partner is about to explode emotionally, I'll have the other partner adopt this open-palm stance. It's a small but powerful reminder that they're not here to hurt each other—they're here to heal and fix things.

## Navigating the "Are You Ready for an Apology?" Gauntlet

When you're gearing up to apologize, asking if your partner is ready to hear it is like playing a game show where the prizes range from a dream vacation to a pie in the face. Here are the four possible responses you might get and how to handle each one like a pro.

## Scenario One: They Say Yes

Congratulations! You've just scored a "yes." This is the equivalent of having your plane cleared for landing. Make sure your seatback is upright and your tray table is stored away because you're halfway to a smooth apology. Proceed with the steps outlined in the next chapter, and try not to do a victory dance until you're completely done.

## Scenario Two: They Say No

If they say no, treat it like they just revealed they've got COVID when we were still calling it the coronavirus. Back away slowly, maybe throw in a "no problem" and let them quarantine in peace. Try again tomorrow when they're not a walking biohazard.

## Scenario Three: They Say "Sure" But Mean "No"

Ah, the classic "sure" that really means "hell no." If their body language is screaming "fight mode," but their mouth says "sure," picture them wrapped up in yellow caution tape. This is an emotional booby trap waiting to explode in your face.

- Visualize the Danger: Think of them as a pit covered with leaves, just waiting for you to step in. It's like they're setting up a POW camp just for you.

- No Easy Outs: Unfortunately, you can't just call them out with, "It doesn't look like you're ready." That's a guaranteed ticket to another week of solitary confinement where your temporary "bad guy" tattoo starts feeling more like an unwanted henna tattoo from a wedding.

Instead, you have to be as smooth as a secret agent.

- Gentle Suggestion: With the calmness of a bomb disposal expert, suggest that it might not seem like they're ready. Maintain a concerned tone and calm body language.

- Reassure and Delay: Ask if they still need time and assure them that it's okay. Say something like, "If the apology is just going to start another fight, it's not fair to either of us."

## Scenario Four: They're Antagonizing Right Away

Sometimes, asking if your partner is ready for an apology is like poking a bear with a stick. You get responses like, "Well, let's see how the apology goes and then I'll let you know," or, "I don't know, what are you apologizing for?" Maybe it's, "If you want to apologize, I'm not going to stop you," or the dreaded, "Is it going to be an apology like last time where you told me how horrible I am?" And then there's the classic, "Nobody's ever ready to say sorry, you just have to do it and see what happens."

In these cases, your partner is throwing a tantrum. Visualize them as a little fat kid demanding a fourth slice of pie. It's not the time to discuss the merits of balanced nutrition; you need to address the tantrum.

Start by saying something like, "It seems like you're still very upset, and understandably so, but I don't think it's fair to either of us if this is going to lead to a bigger fight. I want to help fix the problem and heal our relationship, but if you're not ready, I get it. Why don't I check back in with you in a few hours?"

Usually, they'll either get quiet or fling another combative remark your way. Either way, calmly say, "I love you," and walk away. Let them cool off. When their pulse rate is too high, you have literally zero chance of the apology going well. A different part of their brain has been activated, and they are physically incapable of making amends at this point.

## What If They're Never Ready?

Alright, so you've mastered the art of asking if your partner is ready to hear an apology. But let's be real, nothing is ever that simple in relationships. There are potential challenges that can turn your best-laid plans into a dumpster fire. There's one that is more common than any other that I hear and it's enough to make you want to start climbing the walls looking for an air vent to escape through.

### Dealing with a Partner Who is Never Ready

Sometimes, despite your best efforts, your partner might never seem ready to hear an apology. It's like the old days where we used CDs to listen to music and the deep scratch kept skipping and repeating and then jumping around...even more annoying than a broken record because there was no way for you to lift the needle and move past that part of the vinyl that was flawed. If your partner consistently says they're not ready, it's time to play detective and figure out what's really going on:

1. Communicate Openly: Have a no-b.s. conversation about why they're not ready. Are they still stewing in their emotions? Do they need more time to cool off? Maybe they're secretly plotting your demise.

2. Seek Professional Help: When in doubt, drag in a neutral third party like a couples counselor. Sometimes, you need a referee to call out the fouls and get to the heart of the issue.

3. Be Patient but Persistent: Show that you're committed to making amends and improving the relationship. Keep the lines of communication open without turning into a nagging parrot.

The third option is usually the winning option by the way. It's rare that someone will ask their partner if they're ready to hear an apology consistently for a week straight without hearing a yes. You might want to look in the mirror and ask yourself if maybe you need to practice a little patience. Does it suck to be in the dog house and feel like a stranger in your own home? Sure, but sometimes our screwups mean we're in the dog house and you have to live out the sentence a little and let tempers cool.

Keep in mind that nobody *wants* to stay mad. It's taxing emotionally, mentally and physically. The stress from being in a fight with your partner takes a real toll on people. If there's an alternative route that's usually the one that people will take. Divorce, for example, is almost never done impulsively. There's tons of internal debate and considerations made because we all know instinctively that separation is hard and we don't want to do hard things. Hard things suck!

If there's a nice, warm blanket of an apology waiting for them with a cup of hot cocoa topped with whipped cream and a handful of roasted marshmallows it's just a matter of time until they shyly grab that mug and sidle up to the cozyness. We all want to be loved so keep trying and know you can win over most people with the right attitude and persistence.

**Don't Skip the Ask**

Remember, timing is everything when it comes to apologies. Checking for readiness isn't just about dodging conflict—it's about showing respect and empathy for your partner's emotional state. This small step can lead to more meaningful and effective apologies, ultimately strengthening your relationship.

So, next time you're gearing up to apologize, take a moment to assess the situation. Ask if your partner is ready, respect their response, and be prepared to navigate any challenges that arise. It might not be easy, but it's worth it. Your relationship will thank you for it. Or at least, you'll avoid sleeping on the couch for another night.

# Apology Hall of Shame: Tiger Woods 2009

Timing is everything when it comes to apologies. You have to get the timing right, or you might as well be throwing gasoline on a dumpster fire. Waiting too long to apologize is like waiting until your house is engulfed in flames before you decide to grab a fire extinguisher. This brings us to the legendary debacle of Tiger Woods.

### The Tiger Woods Story: A Perfect Storm of Scandal

Picture this: Tiger Woods, once the golden boy of golf, with more endorsements than you can shake a golf club at, living a life so pristine it made fresh snow look dirty. Tiger Woods wasn't just a golfer; he was *the* golfer. He dominated the sport like a kid hogging the last slice of pizza at a birthday party.

In late November 2009, Woods' image took a nosedive that made Evel Knievel look tame. It all started with a bizarre car crash outside his Florida mansion at 2:30 in the morning. Woods crashed his SUV into a fire hydrant and a tree, which might sound like a bad day, but it was just the opening act.

Soon after, a string of women came forward claiming they had affairs with Woods. It was like someone kicked over an anthill, and suddenly, everyone was spilling the dirt. What followed was a media frenzy that made TMZ look like Pulitzer Prize-winning journalism. Every day, a new mistress, a new scandal, a new headline. Tiger's squeaky-clean image was obliterated faster than you can say "infidelity."

### The Apology: Too Little, Too Late

Tiger Woods decided to address the chaos in February 2010, a full three months after his initial car crash. By this point, the media had roasted him on a spit, and his reputation was already charred to a crisp. Woods held a press conference, but instead of being spontaneous, it looked like a scene from a hostage movie. He apologized, reading from a script, standing stiffly in front of a carefully selected audience of friends and family. It was like watching someone read a eulogy for their career.

Here's the kicker: Tiger's apology was longer than a CVS receipt, it was over 1,500 words long and just about as sincere as a spam email. He talked about being sorry for his actions and the pain he caused, but the whole thing reeked of PR spin. Another issue was he was addressing rumors about performance enhancement drugs or other things about his foundation - that was not the appropriate time to defend yourself. An apology is an apology, don't muddy the water. The delay made it seem like he wasn't genuinely sorry, just sorry he got caught.

## The Public Backlash: A Tornado of Outrage

The public wasn't buying what Tiger was selling. They saw right through the façade. The delayed apology didn't help either; it was like trying to sell ice in Antarctica. Fans felt betrayed, sponsors dropped him faster than a hot potato, and his fellow golfers distanced themselves like he had the plague.

The backlash was brutal. Woods' reputation tanked, his endorsements evaporated, and he became the butt of every late-night joke. People weren't just angry about the affairs; they were furious about the blatant lies and the fact that his apology came after everyone had already made up their minds about him. It was a masterclass in how not to handle a scandal.

In the end, Tiger's delayed apology was about as effective as a screen door on a submarine. It's a stark reminder that timing your apology is crucial. Wait too long, and you might as well be pouring salt on the wound.

## The Apology Tiger Woods Should Have Issued

Imagine a world where Tiger Woods addressed the scandal head-on, with honesty and sincerity, before the media circus took full swing. Here's how that could have looked...and if you're thinking this is long, keep in mind it's just over 400 words and his actual apology was well over three times the length and went off on tangents that didn't even really make sense:

*Good afternoon, everyone. I want to take this opportunity to speak directly to you and address the recent events that have come to light. I owe it to my family, my fans, and my sponsors to be completely honest and open about what has happened.*

*First and foremost, I want to say that I am deeply sorry for my actions. Over the past few years, I have engaged in behavior that is unacceptable, hurtful, and completely contrary to the values I hold dear. I have let down my wife, Elin, my children, my family, and my friends. I have also let down my fans and everyone who has supported me throughout my career.*

*I want to make it clear that I take full responsibility for my actions. There is no excuse for what I have done, and I am not here to make excuses. I am here to apologize and to begin the process of making things right.*

*I have spent the last few days talking to my family, and we are committed to working through this together. I have also started seeking professional help to address the issues that led to my behavior. This is a journey that I need to take for myself, for my family, and for everyone I have hurt.*

*To my fans, I understand that I have disappointed you, and I am truly sorry. I know that words alone are not enough, and I am committed to proving through my actions that I am serious about making amends. I ask for your understanding and patience as I work to rebuild the trust that I have broken.*

*To my sponsors, I apologize for the negative impact my actions have had on our partnerships. I value the relationships we have built over the years, and I am dedicated to earning back your trust and support.*

*Finally, to the media, I understand that you have a job to do. I ask for your respect and privacy as my family and I navigate this difficult time. I will not be discussing the specifics of my behavior further, but I will keep you updated on my progress as I work to make amends.*

*Thank you for listening. I am committed to doing everything in my power to become a better person, a better husband, and a better father. I hope that in time, I can regain your trust and support.*

*Thank you.*

The biggest problem with the actual apology that Tiger Woods delivered was the delay. I think if he got out ahead of it right away his overly long statement might have gone over a little better, even though it wasn't perfect. An apology should have been issued within the first week after the initial car crash and the surfacing of the first rumors. By addressing the issue swiftly and sincerely, Tiger Woods could have taken control of the narrative, shown genuine remorse, and started the process of rebuilding his image before the situation spiraled out of control. Instead we got a taste of the "I'm doing this because I have to" steak served up by the chef's from the PR firm of Condescension and Platitude and most wanted to send it back to the kitchen and just grab a burger at the drive through on the way home.

# 8

# Shut Up and Listen: The Key to Not Sucking at Apologies

THE GOAL OF AN apology is to convey not just remorse, regret, and empathy but to show a sense of transformation that happens inside that little thing you're walking around in that we call a body. What kind of transformation, you might ask? The kind where you're not only going to stop doing the crappy thing you did to piss off your partner, but you've actually changed as a person. You don't even want to do that thing anymore, or you're so cautious about it that you avoid situations where it could even happen.

Let me share a story. One of my clients had a tragic accident where they fell down a flight of stairs while bending over the railing to check out a donut stand below (yes, I did have to hold in my laughter to maintain a professional appearance). After that accident, they didn't just stop bending over railings to look at food stands. They started walking on the other side of the staircase for extra caution. Plus, they began carrying a protein bar to stave off hunger and avoid food temptations altogether (that was my idea).

The goal of an apology is similar: it's not just about stopping the harmful behavior. It's about taking extra steps to ensure it doesn't happen again. To do that, you need to truly transform as a person. How do you do that? It starts with understanding and listening. People think apologizing is all about talking, but surprise—it's not. The real magic happens when you shut that mouth of yours that probably got you in trouble in the first place and open your ears.

Sounds counter intuitive, right? You thought apologizing meant delivering a heartfelt monologue about your remorse, but nope. Unless you're a politician or a PR rep for a celebrity caught in a scandal, you need to throw that script out the window. Real apologies start with listening, not talking. You've got to let the other person unload all their baggage before you can even think about uttering those two little words: "I'm sorry."

So why is this so crucial? Because when you give someone the space to vent, you're showing them that you actually care. You're giving them a platform to air out all their grievances, which helps you understand the full extent of the damage. This isn't just about getting yelled at for a while; it's about really grasping what hurt them, so you can address it properly. It's about empathy, accountability, and making sure your apology doesn't suck.

In this chapter, we're diving into the art of listening—how to do it right and why it's the secret sauce to a killer apology that needs to happen *before* you even try to apologize.

You'll learn how to give the other person the floor, ask the right questions, and make sure they get everything off their chest. Trust me, once you master this, you'll be handing out apologies that actually mend fences instead of setting them on fire.

## Providing Space for the Person to Feel Heard

First things first, you need to create a space where the other person feels comfortable enough to open up. This isn't about dimming the lights and lighting some incense (unless that's your thing). It's about showing them that you're genuinely ready to listen. Ditch the distractions—turn off the TV, put your phone on silent, and for the love of all things holy, don't sneak a peek at your watch. Make it clear that they have your full, undivided attention. Pro tip: consider handing them your phone and saying something like "I don't want this to distract me, would you hold my phone for me?"

**Encouraging Open Communication**

Now, let's get them talking. What you don't want to do is be blunt, obvious, or rushed here. What does this look like? Imagine sitting your partner down, letting out an exasperated sigh that already telegraphs you're against this whole thing, and blurting out, "What do you want me to say sorry for?" Unless your goal is sleeping in separate rooms, this tactic is going to blow up in your face.

You want to telegraph the apology. Dangle it like bait at the end of a hook. You already know they want the apology, so we might as well use that desire to reconnect as the carrot to get them to spill their beans and break down some of those thick walls they've managed to erect around their heart.

What does this sound like? You sit down and, with all the Meryl Streep/Daniel Day-Lewis talent you can muster, you put on a sad face that says you're sorry and worried you've broken the relationship beyond repair. You convey with your eyes and body language that you're scared and concerned. Then you say something like, "I want to apologize for what's happened, but before I do, I want to really understand the full impact of how much I hurt you because I can't imagine what you went through. Tell me all the different ways what I did hurt."

By providing a space where the person feels genuinely heard, you're laying the groundwork for a meaningful apology. It's not just about hearing their words; it's about understanding their feelings and showing that you care enough to give them the floor. This is the first step towards an apology that actually means something.

## The Art of Silence

Depending on your partner, the part where they tell you everything that hurt them might be like pulling teeth, or you might have just opened a floodgate of verbal diarrhea, and you, my friend, are the toilet. Some people just wait their whole life for the complaint department to open up. If you ask them to say all the ways you hurt them, it's like they're finally stepping up to the cash register at a fast-casual restaurant to place their order and they want to customize every little item on the menu and they don't care how many people are in line behind them, it's *their* turn!

In either case, there will be moments of silence. When someone is hurt, they repress a lot of that anger and pain. Pain sucks. Anger sucks. Nobody wants to walk around with it all day. But if they don't have a way to get rid of those icky feelings, they fester without taking any kind of verbal shape inside their head. If they're the verbal diarrhea type, there will be moments where they reshape their pain or recall forgotten moments because now they have a stage to verbalize it, and they want to make sure they get it all out. On the flip side, if they're quiet and resistant, a lot of the silence will be them genuinely struggling to figure out how to verbalize something because that's just not their strong suit.

Resist the urge to help them verbalize. Resist the urge to probe. Resist the urge to speak in general! Silence is golden, especially when it comes to listening. Now, let's face it, silence can be awkward. The trick is to embrace it. Resist, resist, resist. Resist the urge to jump in with your own thoughts or solutions. Just let the silence hang there. The other person will fill it as long as you have your "I'm listening" eyes on and peering into their soul. Words will come, and that's when the real stuff starts to emerge. Interrupting not only breaks their train of thought but also signals that you're more interested in your own opinions than theirs.

Non-verbal cues are your secret weapon here. Channel your inner mime and use body language to show you're engaged. Maintain eye contact, nod thoughtfully, and avoid crossing your arms like a bouncer at a nightclub. Your posture should scream, "I'm all ears!" rather than, "Hurry up, I've got better things to do." Non-verbal cues can make the difference between them feeling heard and them planning your untimely demise.

## Making Sure They Get Everything Off Their Chest

No matter what type of partner you have, eventually, everyone feels uncomfortable telling you what a piece of crap you are if you don't interrupt them. I can't tell you how many times I've been in a couples counseling session and watched as a husband or wife interrupts their partner during a story to "clarify" or defend their actions. Guess what that does? It extends the feeling your partner has of being unimportant to you and prolongs how long they feel justified in turning you into their personal villain.

If people would just shut up, listen, and nod, they'd find that folks aren't super comfortable talking about how horrible someone is when that person is being open-minded and receptive. And it makes sense, right? If you're going to tell someone how selfish and dismissive they are, and the whole time they're being attentive and compassionate, after a few minutes you start to feel like an idiot because the proof that they're not that way is right there.

So the big question is what do you do when they stop talking bad about you? You might be tempted to think that's when you apologize, but nope, now's not the time. Now is the time to double down and get them to say more.

Part of the reason you want to do this is because they will, I promise, feel like they need permission to continue. After all there's a part of them that is being incredibly mean by talking about how horrible you are to your face. They're hurt and the pain may be justified but they can also acknowledge that it's going to make you feel like hot garbage and nobody likes to be the bad guy. But if you're inviting this kind of dialogue as part of the process of healing they'll feel more comfortable continuing.

The other reason that you want to do this is because you want your apology to *fully* heal the problem. We don't really have a great vocabulary when it comes to the infinite spectrum of human emotions that exist. Sometimes we need to talk around a subject hoping we stumble into articulating an idea that has a formless, confusing shape inside of our head. Allowing your partner to stretch and bend this shape until it feels concrete helps them compartmentalize the pain they felt and that's huge. We'll talk more later about this compartmentalization and why it's so crucial.

## Getting to "Enough"

The way you get to the bottom of their grievances is by using two simple questions: "What else?" and "Is that everything?" When they're unloading about all the crap you've done, and you're thinking, "Wow, even I'd hate me if I met this person," it's gonna be tough to keep asking for more. But guess what? Life is about doing the hard stuff.

By inviting your partner to keep going with such a simple, short phrase, you might actually throw them off. Good. Keep pushing. If they roll their eyes, searching for more things to be pissed about, that's a win. You want all the dirt out there. Anytime they seem done talking, just wait a beat and then hit them with, "What else?" Eventually, you'll reach the point where they say, "Nothing," or "That's it, that's everything." Confirm it one more time for good measure. That's when you ask, "Is that everything?"

Sometimes, you'll get a wise-ass response like, "For now." Don't get upset. Smirk and welcome that attitude; it only lowers their defensive walls even more. Say, "No problem. If you think of something else, I'm all ears. But for now, is that everything? As far as what you can think of at this moment, that's everything?"

In case you haven't noticed, your goal is to get a "yes" from them. You want them to say "yes" often during this process so they can realize you're draining them of that pain they've been hoarding. Saying yes, agreeing, and feeling validated is incredibly powerful. So, keep at it until they're out of ammo.

## Handling Emotional Outbursts

Handling emotional outbursts is like dealing with a live grenade—you need to stay calm and composed. If they explode with anger or tears, don't panic. Let them vent. Sometimes, the best response is just to sit there and take it. Show them you can handle their emotions without turning into a deer caught in headlights. Stay supportive, keep your cool, and make a mental note of everything they say, no matter how colorful the language gets.

If during their venting they start bombarding you with questions, don't sweat it. That's normal. Just steer them back to the pain buffet before diving into your side of the story if that's something they actually want to hear. Try something like, "I'm happy to explain why I did it, but first, let's make sure we've got all the pain on the table. I'm guessing it's not just about my reasons but also the mess I've made."

Of course, you're not going to sound like a therapy robot spewing out perfectly articulated responses. You're human, and that's the point. Make it your own, but keep your eye on the prize. Focus on their pain and resist the urge to jump into self-defense mode or cave to their interrogation. The more you listen, the quicker you'll get to the good stuff and start fixing the mess you made. Stay focused, keep it real, and remember: you're not here to win an argument, you're here to clean up the emotional fallout.

## Compartmentalizing the Pain

Compartmentalizing the pain is like organizing a messy garage—sort out the junk so you can see what you're really dealing with. As they've unloaded their emotional baggage, they have really been breaking down the issues into bite-sized pieces. It's like you're sorting through a heap of LEGO bricks, making sure every little grievance is accounted for. This makes the whole mess more manageable and less likely to overwhelm both of you. Plus, it helps prevent those pesky "and another thing" moments during your apology.

## Managing the Infinite Plane of Pain

Emotional pain has this annoying habit of expanding infinitely if you don't contain it. Think of it like a gas leak—you need to seal it off before it fills the room and knocks everyone out. By compartmentalizing their pain, you can put clear boundaries around the pain and the incident. It's like putting up emotional traffic cones to direct the flow of their grievances. This helps to ensure that their pain doesn't spill over into every aspect of your relationship, turning a minor fender bender into a total loss.

If you can get to the place where they say "yes, that's everything," that's when compartmentalizing really starts. They start realizing that the pain their feeling doesn't define the relationship, but is just an unfortunate incident that can be fixed. It separates the pain they're feeling from the way they feel about the relationship as a whole, and that's the essence of why apologies can work.

## Real-Life Example: The Scratched Car

Picture this: you borrowed your friend's brand-new, shiny car, and managed to scratch it while trying to squeeze into a parking spot at a bagel shop that was clearly meant for a bicycle. Let's put aside for a second that it's a poorly designed parking lot that we all suspect was commissioned by the personal injury attorney who happens to own the adjacent storefront.

With deep regret you tell your friend about this accident and with your astute powers of observation and realize your friend looks like they might explode into a thousand tiny angry pieces if you don't flip on the pressure release valve. Your first move? Approach them like you're handling a ticking time bomb. Start with a question, not an apology. "I know you're upset, and I totally get it. Of course, I'm going to fix it and do whatever is needed to repair the damage, but I don't want this to end our friendship. Can you take a moment to tell me what you're feeling right now?" Trust me, this shows you're ready to listen, not just cover your own butt.

## Digging into the Emotional Impact

So, they've started to vent about the scratch. Don't just nod and zone out. Dig deeper. You're an emotional archaeologist, remember? Maybe the scratch isn't just about the scratch. Ask questions that peel back the layers. "Is it just the car, or is there more to it?" They might reveal that this car is their baby, their pride and joy, their midlife crisis purchase that was supposed to bring them endless joy. By understanding the emotional attachment, you're showing that you get the full picture.

## Breaking Down the Layers of Trust Issues

Here's where it gets juicy. As you dig, you discover it's not just about the car's paint job. They feel betrayed because they trusted you with something precious. Now, it's time to compartmentalize. Separate the physical damage from the emotional damage. "I see, so it's not just the scratch, it's that you trusted me and I let you down." This helps you address each issue individually when you eventually apologize, rather than dumping a blanket "I'm sorry" on everything.

Using this example, you've navigated the emotional minefield like a pro. You approached carefully, asked the right questions, dug into the emotional impact, and broke down the layers of trust issues. By doing this, you're not just fixing a scratch; you're repairing a relationship. And when you turn the corner to actually apologize, you'll be able to hit every note perfectly, making your apology as smooth as a brand-new coat of paint.

# Apology Hall of Shame:
# Wells Fargo Fake Accounts 2016

Let me rip open an incident where a company didn't even bother listening to where the pain was coming from. Instead of consulting a single upset customer, they just ran with a generic "our bad" apology that basically told everyone to "get over it." This gem of a move shows exactly why you need to understand the pain before you even think about apologizing.

### The Incident

Alright, buckle up because this one is a doozy. In 2016, Wells Fargo, the bank that loves to tell you they're there to help you reach your financial dreams, got caught with their hand in the cookie jar. Over 5,000 employees had been creating fake bank and credit card accounts without customers' consent. Why? Because they were under insane pressure to meet unrealistic sales targets. Employees were told to hit these targets or hit the road. So, in a desperate bid to keep their jobs, they opened up over two million fake accounts. That's right, two million. Imagine logging into your bank account and seeing a credit card you never signed up for. Surprise!

### The Apology

Enter John Stumpf, the CEO at the time (notice the foreshadowing there), with an apology that missed the mark by a mile. Stumpf did the PR equivalent of throwing a wet blanket on a raging fire. Here's a taste of his groveling, in all its uninspired glory: "We deeply regret and take full responsibility for any such instances and have created a dedicated phone line to ensure any affected customer receives the assistance they need."

Wow, John, way to go. He blamed "unauthorized accounts," making it sound like some rogue employees went on a fun little crime spree without acknowledging the toxic culture of pressure he helped create. It's like apologizing for a burnt dinner without mentioning you set the kitchen on fire.

## The Backlash

The public wasn't buying it, and neither was Congress. The apology was seen as shallow and evasive. People wanted to know why these fake accounts were created in the first place, but Stumpf's apology was like a bad relationship apology where you say, "I'm sorry you're upset," instead of, "I'm sorry I was a jerk." He failed to ask the crucial question: "What exactly hurt you?" and didn't address the broader issues of unethical sales practices and systemic problems within the bank. The backlash was fierce. Customers felt betrayed, employees felt scapegoated, and the public saw it as another example of corporate greed gone wild. Stumpf eventually resigned, but the damage was done. The bank faced massive fines, and their reputation took a nosedive.

## The Better Apology

Now, let's rewrite history and give Wells Fargo an apology that doesn't suck. Here's how Stumpf could have handled it:

*Dear valued customers,*

*I'm John Stumpf, and I'm here to own up to a monumental failure at Wells Fargo. Over two million fake accounts were created by our employees due to the aggressive sales tactics and unrealistic targets set by our leadership, myself included. This was not just a series of unauthorized actions by a few employees; it was a systemic issue fostered by the culture we created.*

*We failed you, and for that, I am deeply sorry. We pressured our employees into unethical behavior, and we betrayed the trust you placed in us. We're not just here to fix these accounts; we're here to rebuild our relationship with you from the ground up.*

*To make things right, we will compensate affected customers and provide free credit monitoring for two years. We're also overhauling our sales practices and implementing new ethical standards to ensure this never happens again. Our entire leadership team, myself included, will be taking a significant pay cut until these issues are resolved.*

*This incident is a clear indication that the relentless pursuit of growth to appease stockholders can lead to unhealthy and unethical practices. We recognize that we've become part of this problem. Moving forward, we are rethinking what growth means for our company. Our focus will shift to providing honest, wholesome customer experiences filled with integrity, even if it means not meeting some unrealistic projection for the stock exchange.*

*I'm not asking for your forgiveness today. I'm asking for the chance to prove that we can do better, and we will. Thank you for giving us the opportunity to make amends.*

## Why it works

This version doesn't just acknowledge the fake accounts; it dives into the root of the problem and takes full responsibility. It shows genuine remorse and offers concrete steps to make things right. It's not about saving face—it's about earning back trust. And that, my friends, is how you turn a corporate disaster into a chance for redemption.

# 9

# Spit It Out! How to Nail Your Apology

YOU'VE MADE IT THIS far without completely screwing up. Congrats. You sat there, probably sweating bullets, while the person you offended unloaded their emotional dump truck on you. They've listed every single way you've messed up, and you've (hopefully) managed to keep your mouth shut and just listen. Now, they've finally admitted that they've gotten everything off their chest. Good for you, you survived. But don't pop the champagne just yet.

### The Importance of Understanding the Pain

Now comes the part where you prove you're not a complete idiot. The most critical step in your apology is showing that you genuinely understand the pain you've caused. This isn't just about nodding like a bobblehead and hoping they'll shut up soon so you can burst out with a "I'm sorry for everything you just said." No, you need to convey that you fully grasp the emotional hurricane you unleashed.

## Comprehending the Pain You Caused

Your apology needs to scream, "I get it!" If your apology doesn't make the other person feel like you truly understand the chaos you've brought into their life, you might as well be apologizing to your toaster. People want to know that you've seen the wreckage, you've walked through the emotional battlefield, and you get how badly you screwed up.

## Why This Understanding is Non-Negotiable

Without this deep understanding, your apology will be about as effective as square wheels on a bicycle. You're trying to make amends, not just cover your own ass. If the person you hurt doesn't believe you truly comprehend their pain, they'll likely toss your "sorry" in the trash and continue plotting your emotional demise to even up the score. And who could blame them?

## The Revenge Prevention Plan

Here's a little secret: when people feel genuinely understood and validated, they don't need to seek revenge. Think of it as a peace treaty in the war zone you created. When they see that you truly get the agony you've caused, they're less likely to dream up creative ways to make you suffer in return. Your goal is to show them that you've taken a front-row seat in their pain theater and you're not just a clueless bystander.

## Parroting the Pain

How do you pull this off? How do you convince them that you're understanding all the yuck inside that they have gone through? You need to regurgitate their complaints back to them, hitting on all the emotional struggles in your own words. Yes, this sounds repetitive, but it's crucial.

You need to be the human echo of their grievances. Only then do you ask the golden question: "Am I understanding everything?" If you get a "yes," you've struck gold. If not, rinse and repeat, my friend. Missing a core part of their pain means you're missing the whole damn point.

## Challenges in Understanding

I'm going to be brutally honest here: you're going to screw this up. Repeatedly. Expect to miss something in this step more often than not. Why? Because human memory is about as reliable as a bio on an online dating site. We think we remember things perfectly, but in reality, our brains are like sieves when it comes to retaining details, especially the ones that make us look bad.

Think about it. How many times have you confidently recalled an event, only to have someone else remind you that you've got it all wrong? Yeah, exactly. Our perception is flawed, and that's putting it mildly. We are terrible witnesses, not just to other people's actions but to our own as well. You probably can't even remember what you had for breakfast last Tuesday, let alone the intricate details of how you messed up someone's day.

This is why, when you're repeating their grievances back to them, you're going to miss something. And when you do, it's going to feel like a punch to the gut because they'll remind you that you still don't get it. But don't panic. This is part of the process. Each mistake is a chance to get closer to a real understanding.

How is this going to work? In practical terms if they say "no" when you ask "did I get everything?" You should ask "what did I miss" or "what part am I leaving out? I want to fully get this from your perspective."

After they repeat what you've missed, repeat everything all over again and ask again "did I get everything?" If they say yes, great, if not, rinse and repeat until you get the yes.

I don't care if you have to do this 20 times, this is the most important part of your whole apology. When they see that you get the pain everything else is easy. This is the part where you have to put in the work. You've already listened to their pain like a hawk, now you have to show them that you were a good witness to their testimony.

Don't feel bad about this. You're diving into the murky waters of human memory and perception. As humans, we just suck at this and there is a mountain of research to back up this idea. Eyewitness testimony is right up there with Bigfoot sightings and UFO abductions. If you want proof look no further than The Innocence Project, those heroes who actually bother with facts and science to exonerate people falsely accused of crimes. They've shown that eyewitness misidentification is the rock star of wrongful convictions. Here's a scary statistic - out of 375 exonerations they helped achieve through DNA, around 70% were because some genius "eyewitness" pointed the finger at the wrong guy.

If you need further convincing, let's talk about some juicy scientific research. Elizabeth Loftus, a rock star in the world of cognitive psychology, has done extensive studies on memory distortion. Her research shows how laughably easy it is to manipulate memories. You think you remember things clearly? Loftus has demonstrated that you can plant entirely false memories in people's minds with just a few suggestive comments. She's proven that our brains are about as reliable as a stripper giving you a genuine compliment.

In one of her famous experiments, Loftus was able to convince people they had seen a car stop at a yield sign when it had actually stopped at a stop sign. Just imagine how easily your memory can be twisted about something as simple as a street sign. Now, consider how much more complex and emotional events can be distorted. This isn't just theory; it's been proven in labs and courts repeatedly.

Or what about the tragic tale of Ronald Cotton. This guy spent 11 years in prison for a crime he didn't commit, all because an eyewitness confidently identified him as the rapist. Jennifer Thompson, the victim, was absolutely sure Cotton was the guy. She picked him out of a lineup and testified against him in court. The jury believed her, because why wouldn't they? After all, eyewitness testimony is supposed to be gold, right? Wrong.

Years later, DNA evidence proved that Cotton was innocent and identified the real perpetrator. Thompson had been dead certain, but she was dead wrong. Her mistake, a simple yet catastrophic error in memory, cost an innocent man over a decade of his life. It's a gut-wrenching example of how unreliable eyewitness testimony can be, even when given with the utmost confidence.

As you navigate the stormy seas of understanding someone else's pain, remember that your memory is about as trustworthy as a politician during election season. You're going to miss details, and that's okay. The key is to keep trying, keep listening, and keep validating until you get it right. Don't stop until you get the "yes." Because, unlike the court of public opinion, in the court of relationships, getting it right is the only verdict that matters.

## Time to Start Actually Apologizing

Here we are, knee-deep in Chapter 8, and only now are we getting to the actual apology. Talk about a marathon just to say "sorry" right. Are we really so terrible that we need to go through all this meditative, voodoo mumbo jumbo just to apologize? Spoiler alert: yes, we are. I've seen a well-executed apology make someone call off the divorce lawyers and a bad one make them pack their bags and move out that night.

I'm going to break down the verbal apology into seven distinct categories so you can blend all these ingredients into a smoothie that goes down nice and smooth. Don't start sweating bullets thinking this is going to be like memorizing the Gettysburg Address. In an ideal world, you'll nail all of these, but even if you only hit 50%, it'll still be worlds better than where you are now. And in my book, improvement is improvement.

And don't worry, I'm not just going to leave you hanging with a bunch of abstract steps. After I break down these seven crucial components of a killer apology, I'll hit you with a few real-world examples. Think of it as the highlight reel of apologies—so you can see what it looks like when all the parts are strung together in glorious harmony. Stick with me, and by the end, you'll be apologizing like a pro, or at least not like a total disaster.

**First Part: Owning Your Screw-Up**

Time to face the music. The first step in not being a total waste of space is owning your screw-up. This means taking full, unfiltered responsibility for the mess you've made. No passing the buck to your childhood trauma, the weather, or Mercury being in retrograde. It's all on you, champ. The person you've royally pissed off needs to hear you say, "I caused this pain." No one else, just you. This shows that you're not an immature brat dodging blame but someone who actually gets the magnitude of their own idiocy.

Why is this so damn important? Because without taking responsibility, your apology is about as useful as a dead cell phone on a rescue mission. The person you've hurt doesn't want to hear your sad excuses or half-baked justifications. They want to know you understand the impact of your actions. By saying you alone are responsible, you show you're not trying to weasel out of accountability, which is a non-negotiable if you ever hope to rebuild trust.

**Second Part: Admitting the Betrayal**

Next up, admit you've screwed them over and shattered their trust. This is where you spill your guts: "I made a mistake, I betrayed your trust, and I hurt you." Get specific about what you did wrong. None of that vague "I'm sorry for everything" crap. They need to hear that you understand exactly what you did to mess up the relationship. By being specific, you show that you're not glossing over the ugly details. The good news is that you can reference all the stuff you got the "yes" for earlier so this should be a cake walk.

Why is this step so vital? Because it acknowledges the emotional grenade you lobbed into their life. It's not just about the physical or tangible consequences; it's about the emotional betrayal. This step helps the person you hurt see that you're fully aware of the extent of your actions and their repercussions. It's about validating their feelings and proving that you recognize the breach of trust.

### Third Part: Expressing Genuine Regret

Now comes the part where you let the guilt wash over you like a wave of tequila-induced nausea. You need to convey your remorse in a way that shows you're genuinely devastated by what you've done. Use words like "devastated," "ashamed," "mortified," "embarrassed," and "humiliated." You've got to make it crystal clear that the guilt is gnawing at your soul and that you truly understand the pain you've caused.

Why is expressing genuine regret so crucial? Because it helps the person you hurt see that you're not brushing this off. It shows that you're emotionally invested in making things right. When you can convey the depth of your regret, it bridges the emotional chasm created by your actions. This isn't just about mouthing "sorry"; it's about making them feel your sorrow and remorse down to their core.

### Fourth Part: Showing Time Machine Regret

Time for a little time-travel fantasy. You need to make it clear that if you could rewind the clock, you'd do everything differently. Paint a vivid picture of how you'd avoid being such a monumental screw-up. Tell them you deeply regret causing them pain and wish you could undo it. This shows that you've thought about the consequences of your actions and would take steps to avoid them in the future.

Why is this so important? Because it ties your apology to their pain. It's not just about feeling bad; it's about wishing you'd made better choices. This step reinforces your understanding of the hurt you caused and your desire to make things right. It helps the person you hurt see that you're committed to avoiding such colossal blunders in the future.

## Fifth Part: Reaffirming Relationship Value

Admit it: your actions made them question how much you value the relation-ship. This is where you acknowledge the ultimate sin: making them doubt their importance to you. Say something like, "I made you question our relationship's value to me, and that's the worst thing I could have done." Then, reaffirm how much you care and how important they are to you.

Why is this step essential? Because it addresses the core of their hurt. They need to know that despite your screw-ups, you value them and the relationship deeply. This step helps to rebuild the emotional connection and shows that you're committed to making things right. It's about repairing the emotional breach and proving that you understand the significance of what you've jeop-ardized.

## Sixth Part: Committing to Change

Finally, make a solid commitment to change. Detail the steps you're going to take to ensure you don't repeat your idiocy. Whether it's therapy, self-help books, or some other form of personal development, make it clear that you're serious about improving. Say something like, "I promise to never let this happen again. I'm going to start [specific action] to make sure I change."

Why is this so important? Because it shows that you're not just blowing smoke about wanting to improve. It demonstrates that you're willing to put in the effort to ensure that your apology is more than just hot air. By outlining specific steps, you show that you're dedicated to making lasting changes to prevent future hurt. This final step is what helps to rebuild trust and ensures that your apology leads to real, meaningful change.

## Seventh Part: Making Restitution

Here's the deal: if you break it, you buy it. This is the seventh part of your apolo-gy, and it's all about making restitution. This means if you broke something, you better offer to replace it. If you wasted their time, figure out a way to make it up to them. If you threw an insult their way, it's time to pull out the compliments.

Why is this important? Because actions speak louder than words, my friend. It's one thing to say "I'm sorry," but it's another thing entirely to show you mean it. So, if you smashed their favorite mug in a fit of rage, get your butt to the store and buy a new one. If you blew off a date to binge-watch Netflix, clear your schedule and plan a special outing to make up for it. And if you called them a name in the heat of the moment, start laying on the genuine compliments.

Restitution isn't just about fixing what you broke; it's about showing you're willing to go the extra mile to make things right. It's a tangible way to demonstrate that you value the relationship and are committed to repairing the damage. So, roll up your sleeves and put in the effort. It's not rocket science, but it does take a bit of thought and a lot of sincerity. Think of it as the cherry on top of your apology sundae—without it, you're just serving up plain old vanilla, and nobody's impressed by that.

Now let's break down three different scenarios and the apology that could come after so you can understand how this all works in real-world scenarios.

## Scenario 1: Financial Disagreements

Meet Alex and Jamie, the poster children for financial incompatibility. Alex, a budgeting wizard with a spreadsheet fetish, nearly has a coronary every time Jamie makes an impulse purchase. Picture this: Jamie waltzes in one day, grinning like a Cheshire cat, because she bought a $2,500 massage chair. Alex's eyes nearly bug out of his head as he imagines their savings account gasping for air.

"Are you serious? We're supposed to be saving for a house, and you blow a $2,500 on...this?!" Alex explodes as he stares at the monstrosity of expense and luxury they can't afford.

Jamie, feeling more misunderstood than a mime at a rap battle, fires back, "It's my money too! I'm not asking permission to spend it!"

Their argument devolves into a shouting match, each accusing the other of being irresponsible or controlling, with the poor gadget caught in the crossfire.

Jamie eventually takes the steps to understand why Alex was bothered and then offers a great apology:

## Owning Your Screw-Up

"Okay, I screwed up. I bought that expensive gadget without talking to you, and that was irresponsible. I caused this financial strain, and I own that."

## Admitting the Betrayal

"I betrayed your trust by making a major purchase without discussing it. You needed to feel secure about our financial future, and I let you down."

## Expressing Genuine Regret

"I'm devastated and ashamed. I see now how much stress this caused you, and I regret it deeply."

## Showing Time Machine Regret

"If I could rewind, I'd never have bought that gadget without a conversation. I'd prioritize our goals and our financial stability over my impulse buys."

## Reaffirming Relationship Value

"My actions made you question how much I value our relationship, and that's the worst thing I could have done. You and our future and buying a house together mean everything to me."

## Committing to Change

"I promise to never make such a significant purchase without discussing it with you first. I'm going to start a monthly budget meeting so we're always on the same page financially."

## Making Restitution

"I'm returning the gadget and putting that money back into our savings. To make up for this, I'll also plan a date night where we don't spend a dime, so we can enjoy each other's company without financial stress."

## Scenario 2: Division of Household Chores

Meet Lisa and Mark, the dynamic duo of domestic dysfunction. Both work full-time, but when it comes to housework, they're as synchronized as a cat and a dog. Lisa returns home, exhausted from her job, to find the kitchen looking like a tornado hit it and the kids still dirty from their day's adventures.

"Seriously, Mark? You couldn't even get the kids a bath or clean up this mess?" Lisa snarls, her frustration bubbling over like an overfilled washing machine.

Mark, having spent the afternoon fixing the garage door (again), shoots back, "Oh, come on! I did the yard work and fixed the garage door! How is that not helping?"

Their evening spirals into a battle royale over who does more, each convinced they're the unsung hero of the household. Eventually Mark realized he screamed too loud and too harshly at his wife and sat down with Lisa to hear her out and get to the apology which sounded like this:

### Owning Your Screw-Up

"I messed up by not helping more with the kids and the house. I caused this imbalance, and that's on me."

### Admitting the Betrayal

"I betrayed your trust by not sharing the load equally. You needed support, and I dropped the ball."

### Expressing Genuine Regret

"I feel mortified and ashamed that you've been carrying so much of the burden. I'm sorry for making you feel unappreciated."

### Showing Time Machine Regret

"If I could go back, I'd have jumped in to help with the kids and cleaned the kitchen. I'd make sure you never felt alone in this."

### Reaffirming Relationship Value

"My actions made you question how much I value our partnership, and that's unforgivable. You and our family mean the world to me."

### Committing to Change

"I'm committed to changing. I'll start by taking on more daily chores and making sure we split the workload evenly. Let's create a chore schedule together."

**Making Restitution**

"I'm taking over the evening routine for the next week, so you can relax. And this weekend, I'm planning a special family day where you don't have to lift a finger."

## Scenario 3: Different Parenting Styles

Say hello to Sara and Tom, the parents locked in a never-ending battle of parenting philosophies. Their teenage son, Jake, brings home a science project report that got a big fat 35% on it - way to go, Jake! Totally his fault, by the way - he got sucked into Fortnite for the last two months and phoned in the report the night before. Sara wants to talk it out calmly; Tom's ready to ground him until he's 30.

"Ground him? Are you kidding me, Tom? He needs understanding, not a prison sentence!" Sara fumes, her voice rising.

Tom, channeling his inner drill sergeant, snaps back, "Understanding? He needs discipline! He's not going to learn if we keep coddling him!"

The argument escalates, each accusing the other of either being too harsh or too lenient, with poor Jake stuck in the middle, probably wishing he'd been born into another family. Eventually Tom calls Sara some pretty bad names and throws harsh words at Tom that are as hard to walk back as an unwanted pregnancy. The mud slinging got out of hand and Tom realized he just took it way too far. He was able to cool off and get Lisa to talk to him enough to get ready to offer a proper apology:

**Owning Your Screw-Up**

"I was wrong to push my strict approach without considering your perspective. I lost control of my temper and said things I didn't mean that hurt both you and Tom. I caused this conflict, and it's my fault."

### Admitting the Betrayal

"I betrayed your trust by not respecting your parenting style. You needed us to be a united front, and I failed."

### Expressing Genuine Regret

"I'm embarrassed and ashamed that I made you feel unheard and unsupported. I deeply regret causing this rift."

### Showing Time Machine Regret

"If I could go back, I'd listen to your viewpoint and find a balanced approach. I'd make sure we presented a united front to Jake."

### Reaffirming Relationship Value

"My actions made you question our partnership in parenting, and that's the last thing I wanted. You and our family are my top priority."

### Committing to Change

"I promise to work with you on our parenting strategy. I'm committed to regular discussions about how we handle issues with Jake, so we're always on the same page. And I'm going to take up meditation like we spoke about earlier to try to rein in some of that anger."

### Making Restitution

"I'll take the lead on Jake's next school project, making sure we support him together. And I'm setting up a family meeting so we can all discuss our expectations and rules moving forward."

Now that we've gone over three different situations where you've heard great apologies that really tick all of the boxes, let's turn to one of my favorite parts where we see the trainwrecks that happen in such an excruciatingly public way.

# Apology Hall of Shame: BP Oil Spill 2010

Let me take you back to 2010, the year when BP decided to redefine what it means to screw up royally. On April 20th, the Deepwater Horizon oil rig exploded in the Gulf of Mexico, unleashing a torrent of crude oil that gushed unabated for 87 days. It was an environmental catastrophe of epic proportions. Birds, fish, and marine life were suddenly auditioning for the lead role in the latest dystopian disaster flick. Local fishermen watched helplessly as their livelihoods went up in oily smoke, and beaches transformed into tar pits.

As if the environmental Armageddon wasn't enough, enter Tony Hayward, the CEO of BP at the time. A man whose PR skills could rival a dumpster fire. In the midst of the chaos, when emotions were high, and the world was watching, he totally threw up an airball in the apology world.

## The Failed Apology

Tony Hayward's apology is a masterclass in how not to say you're sorry. His statement, delivered with all the sincerity of a wet mop, was as follows:

*"There's no one who wants this thing over more than I do. I'd like my life back."*

Where do we start? First, the apology centers around him—a colossal mistake. The people suffering, losing their jobs, and witnessing environmental devastation don't give a flying fish about Hayward's inconveniences. This was a textbook case of poor empathy, lack of understanding, and downright tone-deafness. While the Gulf Coast was dealing with an ecological apocalypse, Hayward's biggest grievance was his disrupted lifestyle.

To be fair it wasn't a press briefing, it was just a candid interview by the harbor and he was talking about all the things being done to try to fix it but it slipped out and was in incredibly poor taste - not to mention showed his true colors which revealed a complete lack of accountability or any kind of effort at a true internal transformation. That one clip was on repeat on all the news stations over and over and over again for days

## The Backlash

The public's reaction was swift and brutal. The comment sparked outrage across the globe. Hayward's words became the embodiment of corporate insensitivity. The media had a field day, social media platforms erupted with fury, and BP's stock took a nosedive. Memes flourished, depicting Hayward as the poster boy for corporate greed and apathy. There were calls for his resignation, and BP's already tarnished reputation sank faster than the Titanic.

## The Better Apology

So, how could Tony Hayward have avoided his VIP seat in the Apology Hall of Shame? Here's what a great apology might have looked like:

*Good evening. I am Tony Hayward, CEO of BP. I stand before you today deeply saddened and profoundly sorry for the catastrophic events following the Deepwater Horizon explosion. The devastation to the Gulf Coast's environment, the impact on the livelihoods of so many families, and the loss of eleven brave workers is truly heart-wrenching.*

*Our responsibility is immense, and our response will be equally substantial. We are committed to taking full accountability for this disaster. We will spare no resources in our efforts to clean up the spill, restore the affected areas, and support the communities and ecosystems that have been impacted.*

*I want to personally assure you that BP will not rest until we have made amends for this tragedy. Our focus is not on our own inconveniences but on the immense suffering and disruption caused by our actions. We will work tirelessly with local, state, and federal authorities to ensure comprehensive and transparent efforts in addressing this crisis.*

*To the families who have lost loved ones, to those whose livelihoods have been shattered, and to everyone affected by this disaster, I am truly sorry. Our commit-*

*ment to you is unwavering, and we will strive to earn back your trust through our actions in the coming days, months, and years. Thank you.*

By acknowledging the gravity of the situation, expressing genuine empathy, and outlining a concrete plan for restitution, Hayward could have transformed his apology from a PR disaster into a step toward redemption. Instead, his words will forever be a cautionary tale of how not to apologize. Not to mention a meme-worthy clip that I'm sure some of his friends still text him to this day when they're late to dinner.

# 10

# Please Forgive Me... Pretty Pretty Please!

So, you've managed to choke out an apology. Bravo. Maybe you even threw in some restitution, confessed your sins, and made the whole process more awkward than a middle school dance. But guess what? You're not done yet. There's one more step that most people conveniently "forget": actually asking for forgiveness. Yeah, I said it. You have to *ask*.

Why is this so hard for people to grasp? Probably because it's like voluntarily jumping into a shark tank. You're putting yourself at the mercy of the person you wronged, and that's terrifying. But let's get real. If you don't ask for forgiveness, you're not really apologizing. You're just throwing words at a problem and hoping they stick.

Let's break it down: verbalizing the ask for forgiveness is crucial. It's the part that forces you to be vulnerable and admit that you might not be off the hook. It's the part where you stop tap dancing around your screw-up and face it head-on. Skipping this step is like baking a cake and forgetting the sugar—sure, you've got something that looks like a cake, but nobody's gonna want to eat it.

Common misconceptions? People think forgiveness is implied. "Oh, I said I'm sorry, and they nodded, so we're good." Nope. That's not how it works. Assuming forgiveness is there without asking for it is like assuming you're a great dancer just because no one's told you otherwise. Trust me, they're talking about your terrible moves behind your back. So, do everyone a favor and just ask. It's not that hard. Or maybe it is, but tough luck. It's necessary.

## Making it clear, no exceptions

Alright, let's get one thing straight: assuming forgiveness is the lazy person's way out. You might think, "I apologized, so they must have forgiven me," but that's just you avoiding the hard part. Let's look at some examples of weak apologies that fail to ask for forgiveness. Picture this: "I'm sorry for what I did, okay? Can we just move on?" This is about as effective as trying to put out a fire with a teaspoon of water. You're not addressing the hurt you caused; you're just taping a piece of paper over a hole in a wall and hoping nobody notices.

But why is making it clear so important? Because it leaves no room for ambiguity. When you assume forgiveness, you're leaving a massive elephant in the room. The other person might still be hurt, angry, or confused, but you're acting like everything's fine. By asking for forgiveness, you're inviting an honest dialogue. It's like saying, "I know I messed up, and I'm here to make it right. Tell me what you need." It's a gesture of respect and humility, which, let's face it, is probably the last thing on your mind when you're apologizing. But it's necessary. Without it, your apology is half-baked at best.

This clarity also helps prevent future misunderstandings. When you ask for forgiveness and receive it, both parties are on the same page. There's a mutual acknowledgment of the mistake and the forgiveness given. It's a clean slate, a fresh start. Without this, you're left with lingering doubts and unresolved feelings that can fester and lead to more problems down the road. So, stop being lazy. Make it clear. Ask for forgiveness. Your relationships will thank you for it.

## The Healing Process

Alright, let's get one thing straight. Forgiveness is the duct tape that holds the cracked, dysfunctional pieces of a relationship together. When you ask for forgiveness, you're not just looking for a "get out of jail free" card. You're jumpstarting a healing process that's been limping along like a three-legged dog. Imagine trying to run a marathon with a sprained ankle. That's what it's like trying to patch up a relationship without forgiveness. You're just hobbling along, making a fool of yourself.

Forgiveness is the ultimate emotional band-aid. Without it, the wound stays open, festering with all kinds of nasty resentment and anger. When you ask for forgiveness, you're helping to slap that bandage on. Sure, it might still sting like hell, and the scar might stay forever, but at least it's on the mend. Healing allows both of you to stop living in the past and start looking at something that resembles a future.

Remember, forgiveness doesn't mean wiping the slate clean. It doesn't mean what happened was okay. It means you're willing to let go of the rage and bitterness to make space for something better. When you ask for forgiveness, you're acknowledging the epic screw-up and offering a way forward. It's not just about making you feel better; it's about helping the person you wronged to heal. And that, my friends, is the real kicker.

## Forgiveness in Action

Let's dig into a real-life story that turned around after a proper ask for forgiveness from actual patients of mine, Grace and Andrew:

"He's said sorry before, but I don't believe it," Grace spat, her eyes flashing with a mix of anger and exhaustion. She looked like she was ready to throw Andrew out the window. Andrew, her husband, slumped next to her, looking like he wanted to melt into the floor.

Grace and Andrew were an Armenian couple. Andrew always wore a gold cross necklace that hovered over the open collar of his button-down shirt. His slicked-back hair and expensive shoes completed his meticulously polished look. Grace, on the other hand, preferred comfortable, flowy outfits that, despite their relaxed appearance, clearly came with hefty price tags. Her makeup was always impeccable, making it all the more heartbreaking to see her cry in our sessions. She constantly blotted her tears, trying to prevent her face from turning into a puddle of eyeliner and foundation.

"Grace, enlighten me. Why don't you believe his apologies?" I asked, not bothering to mask my sarcasm.

Grace rolled her eyes. "It's not that I don't believe his apologies. I believe he regrets what he did. But regret isn't enough. He's never made any real effort to fix what he broke. He yells, he says sorry, and then expects everything to go back to normal. My dad is proud and stubborn. He's been avoiding family gatherings for months now because of Andrew's outburst. I talk to him every day, and he's still so hurt. Every time Andrew apologizes, it's like he's reading off a script."

I leaned in. "Tell me more about what happened that day, Grace."

She took a deep breath. "It was our anniversary party. Everyone was there, and everything was perfect until my dad started making those comments about Andrew's job. He kept saying Andrew wasn't providing for me properly, and it just escalated. Andrew snapped and yelled at him in front of everyone. My dad was humiliated and stormed out. Since then, he's refused to come to any family events if Andrew is there."

Andrew finally raised his head. "I know I screwed up, but your dad kept making those snide remarks about my job, and I just snapped. I've apologized a million times, Grace. What do you want from me? Blood?"

Grace glared at him. "It's not about just saying sorry, Andrew. My dad needs to see that you're really sorry, that you're willing to actually do something about it."

I sighed, feeling the tension rise. "Okay, so your father needs action, not just empty words. Andrew, any bright ideas on how you can show you're serious?"

Andrew scratched his head, thinking. "Well, your dad's been moaning about that chandelier in the guest room for ages. He wants to replace it with a ceiling fan but has no clue how to do it. I could offer to help him with that. It's practical, and it shows I'm willing to get my hands dirty to make things right."

Grace's face softened slightly, but she still looked skeptical. "Maybe. He does respect people who can actually do something useful. But this has to be your thing, Andrew, not mine."

I leaned back, crossing my arms. "Alright, so we have a plan. Andrew, you're going to put your handyman skills to use and help your father-in-law with the ceiling fan. Grace, you're going to give him a chance to show he's serious. It's not going to be a walk in the park, but it's a start."

Andrew nodded. "I can do that. I'll call him tomorrow and offer to help."

Grace looked at him, a hint of relief in her eyes. "Thank you, Andrew."

I wasn't done yet. "Andrew, tell me more about your frustration that day. What exactly did your father-in-law say to set you off?"

Andrew sighed, rubbing his temples. "He kept making those passive-aggressive comments about my job. He said I wasn't providing well enough for Grace, that I wasn't a real man. It felt like a knife twisting in my gut. I lost control and yelled at him. I know it was wrong, but I felt so cornered."

Grace nodded, her eyes softening a bit. "I know my dad can be difficult. He has his ways, and he's proud. But yelling at him in front of everyone wasn't the answer."

Andrew looked down. "I understand that now. But every time I've tried to apologize, he just brushes me off. It's like nothing I say matters."

I saw an opening. "Grace, what do you think it will take for your father to start mending this rift?"

Grace took a moment to think. "He respects actions more than words. If Andrew helps him with the ceiling fan, it will show that he's serious about making amends. My dad values people who can do practical things, who can actually fix problems."

Andrew nodded. "I can do that. I'll show him I'm willing to make things right."

"Good," I said. "Now, Andrew, I want you to repeat your apology to Grace, but this time, include your plan for fixing things."

Andrew turned to Grace, his eyes earnest. "Grace, I'm truly sorry for yelling at your father. I know I hurt you and him, and I regret it deeply. I want to make things right. I'll help him with the ceiling fan, and I'll do whatever it takes to mend this rift."

Grace's eyes softened further. "Thank you, Andrew. That means a lot to me."

"Andrew," I continued, "I think it's important to ask for her forgiveness."

Andrew took a deep breath. "Grace, will you forgive me?"

She smiled slightly. "If you help my dad with the ceiling fan, I'm sure he'll soften. And yes, I'd be happy and eager to forgive you then."

As they embraced in a hug and kiss, I felt a sense of hope. If Andrew could follow through, they had a real chance at patching things up. And if not, at least they'd have a new ceiling fan.

Andrew's revised apology was a masterclass in not screwing up for once. Instead of the usual half-hearted, "I'm sorry," he actually proposed a concrete plan. It's shocking, I know—an apology with a real solution attached. Helping with the ceiling fan? Genius. It's practical, it's hands-on, and it's exactly what Grace's dad respects. Andrew finally understood that actions speak louder than words, and his willingness to get his hands dirty showed he was ready to back up his words with real effort. For a guy who usually couldn't find his way out of a paper bag, this was a monumental step forward.

But the real kicker? Grace's willingness to forgive. Let's be real here—her forgiveness was the magic sauce that made this whole thing work. Without it, Andrew's apology would've just been another shout into the void. Grace didn't just want words; she needed to see Andrew's regret in action. And when she saw that, she was ready to meet him halfway. Her forgiveness wasn't some passive, "Okay, I guess it's fine." It was an active decision to move forward together. It created a path for reconciliation that words alone could never pave. So yeah, Andrew's apology was better, but it was Grace's willingness to forgive that truly pushed them toward mending their relationship. The proof was in the hug and kiss embrace that happened immediately after as a sign of hope that they aren't going to continue punishing each other for this unfortunate incident.

## What if Forgiveness Isn't Offered?

So, you've mustered up the courage to ask for forgiveness, and you're met with a resounding "no." Or worse, silence. Now what? Handle that rejection with some grace, my friend. Acting like a toddler who just got their favorite toy taken away isn't going to win you any points. This is where you dig deep and find that last shred of humility.

First off, if forgiveness isn't offered right away, don't freak out. Not everyone is ready to hand out forgiveness like it's candy on Halloween. People need time to process their feelings, and your job is to respect that. This isn't about you anymore; it's about them. So, if you hear "I need time" or "I can't forgive you right now," take a deep breath and back off. Give them space. The last thing you want to do is pressure them into forgiving you. That's not forgiveness; that's coercion.

But here's the kicker: when forgiveness isn't granted, it's your chance to ask, "What do you need from me to be able to forgive?" Yeah, it sounds like you're setting yourself up for more groveling, but this is crucial. It shows that you're committed to making things right, not just looking for a quick fix. Maybe they need you to prove you've changed. Maybe they need a grand gesture. Or maybe they just need time to cool down. Whatever it is, asking this question puts the ball in their court and shows you're willing to do the hard work.

Let's be real, sometimes forgiveness isn't immediate, and sometimes it's never going to come. That's a bitter pill to swallow, but it's reality. You can't control how someone else feels. If they're not ready or willing to forgive, respect that decision. You've done what you can by asking. Now it's on them. Your job is to continue being a better person and to prove through your actions that you've truly changed. Sometimes, that's all you can do. The funny thing is that people get this. I can't tell you how many times I've had a couple where they work through the apology and they can't forgive and then the offended partner calls me to have a little one on one asking me how they can let go because they want to forgive but can't. They actually recognize that it's their own problem now and it's usually a pretty interesting journey for them to learn how to move forward.

In the end, forgiveness is a two-way street. You've got to ask for it, and they've got to be willing to give it. If it doesn't happen right away, don't lose hope. Keep working on yourself and showing them that you're worth forgiving. It's a long game, but the payoff is worth it.

In all my years working with married couples I've never seen anyone fail at apologizing and forgiveness, just give up. I promise that if you throw someone a dismissive apology and expect everything to be back to normal five minutes later you're dreaming, but I also promise that if you're willing to apologize everyday for the next ten years and back it up with action I'm sure at some point your partner will forgive you.

Does it usually take ten years? No. And if it does I would check your partner for severe amnesia or something because there's a wire that's been crossed. Somewhere between five minutes and ten years everyone can learn to forgive. Usually I find for most things it takes a few hours to a couple of weeks. The exceptions are in the very egregious cases like cheating or bankrupting a family. Even in those cases, however, a year is usually the sentence that's carried out for being able to come off the bench and play again.

## Repeated Offenses

So, you've managed to mess up more than once. Congratulations, you're officially on the "serial screw-up" list. Asking for forgiveness when you've made multiple mistakes isn't just hard—it's damn near impossible. But guess what? You still have to do it. Skipping this step because it's tough is like deciding not to shower because you're too dirty. It's a self-defeating cycle.

First, let's talk about how to ask for forgiveness if you've screwed up more than once. You need to acknowledge the pattern of behavior. Something like, "I know I've hurt you before, and I've done it again. I can't tell you how sorry I am. Can you forgive me?" This shows that you're not just sweeping the past under the rug. You're owning up to the fact that you've been a repeat offender. It's brutal honesty, and it's necessary.

Next, you've got to prove that you're serious about changing. Words are cheap, especially when you've used them over and over to apologize for the same damn thing. This is where actions speak louder than words. Start showing, not just telling, that you're making a real effort to change. If you're always late, start being early. If you're always forgetting important dates, set a million reminders. Do whatever it takes to break the cycle of your crappy behavior.

Rebuilding trust after multiple apologies is like trying to rebuild a house of cards in a wind tunnel. It's delicate, and one wrong move can bring the whole thing crashing down. Consistency is key. You can't just be good for a week and expect everything to be fine. You've got to keep it up. Day in and day out, show through your actions that you're committed to being a better person. And for the love of all that's holy, stop making the same mistakes. Learn from them. Even if the mistake is small, like neglecting to clean up the house for the fifteenth time. Snap out of it!

I wish they had a twelve step program for husbands who keep forgetting to do the dishes. They would all meet wearing dish gloves and have a solemn oath they take, "God, I swear to view all dishes as dirty until clean and view my wife as healthy instead of OCD. Baseboards need to be dusted, clothing doesn't belong on the floor, and sweeping and mopping are both necessary. I can change with your help and in the name of Pine Sol, Dawn, and Tide we pray for your guidance." Why am I wasting my time writing this book with a million dollar idea like that?

You also need to communicate openly about what you're doing to change. Let the person you've wronged know the steps you're taking to ensure you don't mess up again. It's like a parole hearing—show that you've reformed and aren't just going to fall back into old habits. This transparency helps rebuild trust because it shows you're not just trying to sweep your past offenses under the rug. You're actively working to be better.

In the end, asking for forgiveness after repeated offenses is about proving that you're capable of change. It's about showing that you're not just saying sorry out of habit, but because you genuinely want to make things right. It's a long, hard road, and there are no guarantees. But if you're committed to doing the work, there's a chance you can earn that forgiveness and start to rebuild what you've broken. Just remember, consistency and honesty are your best friends here. Don't let them down.

## When Forgiveness is Delayed

So you've done the hard part. You've apologized, asked for forgiveness, and even made restitution. And then you wait. And wait. And nothing. The silence is deafening, and your anxiety is through the roof. Welcome to the waiting game, where forgiveness isn't granted on your timeline but on theirs. And here's the kicker—you have to be okay with that.

First things first, patience is your new best friend. When forgiveness is delayed, it's easy to get frustrated and feel like your efforts are for nothing. But let's get real: not everyone processes their emotions at the same speed. Some people need time to let go of the anger, the hurt, and the betrayal. Your job is to respect their process. If they say they need time, give them time. If they're not ready to forgive, don't push it. Pushing for forgiveness is like trying to speed up a sloth—it's not going to happen, and you'll just end up looking like an idiot.

But while you're waiting, don't just sit there twiddling your thumbs. Use this time to show through your actions that you're serious about making things right. Be consistent in your behavior. Keep doing the things you promised to do to make amends. If you said you'd communicate better, then start being a communication ninja. If you said you'd be more reliable, then show up like clockwork. This isn't about proving you're worthy of forgiveness; it's about being a better person, period.

Now, let's talk about how to support the offended party while they process their feelings. You might think, "I've apologized, what more do they want?" The answer: more. They want to see that you're not just in it for a quick fix but are genuinely committed to their well-being. This means being there for them without being overbearing. Check in on them, but don't hover. Offer support, but don't smother. It's a fine line, but if you truly care, you'll figure it out.

And here's a tough pill to swallow: sometimes, forgiveness might never come. That's right. You could do everything perfectly and still not get the forgiveness you're seeking. People have their own journeys and traumas, and sometimes the hurt is just too deep. If that's the case, you have to accept it. It doesn't mean you stop being a better person. It doesn't mean you revert to your old ways. It means you respect their decision and continue to live in a way that reflects your growth and change.

In the end, delayed forgiveness is a test of your patience and commitment. It's about proving that you're not just looking for a quick way out but are genuinely invested in making things right. Keep showing up, keep doing the work, and most importantly, keep respecting their process. Forgiveness, if it comes, will be worth the wait. And if it doesn't, at least you can say you did everything in your power to make amends. And that, my friend, is what true growth looks like.

To scratch that itch a little harder, let's take a look at someone who never offers forgiveness. If you've done the work. If you've followed all of these steps and heard your partner out, repeating their pain, apologized and asked for forgiveness and they say no and then you follow through with actions consistently for months or a year, then you have my permission to forgive yourself.

If someone is still holding on to something and can't seem to let go in the face of a transformation the problem is theirs now, not yours. It sometimes does mean that you won't be together, not all things in relationships are fixable, but you do need to relieve yourself of the burden of carrying around the weight of your wrongdoings at some point. It's not fair. Life is too short and if you've changed, take solace in the fact that you are a new person and the one who committed the transgression that got your partner's panties tied up in a knot was a different you. If they can't see that, it's not your problem (but that's assuming you've actually done the work and aren't just using that as a get out of jail free card while still being the same screw-up who made the mistake).

# Apology Hall of Shame:
# Uber's Various Scandals 2017

Another chapter means another chance to wind back the clock and gaze open-mouthed at the head-on collision of an apology that happened in the public eye not too long ago. Let's dive into the Uber train wreck of 2017. Uber, the ride-hailing behemoth, managed to steer itself straight into a series of scandals that would make even the most hardened corporate execs cringe. It all started with a blog post by former Uber engineer Susan Fowler, who blew the lid off the company's toxic culture. Her account detailed rampant sexual harassment, gender discrimination, and a management that turned a blind eye to complaints.

But wait, there's more! As if the sexual harassment revelations weren't enough, Uber was also exposed for a host of unethical practices. These included "Greyball," a program designed to evade authorities, and allegations of stealing trade secrets from Google's self-driving car project. Oh, and let's not forget the high-profile video of Uber CEO Travis Kalanick berating an Uber driver. In short, Uber was a hot mess, and the world was watching.

## The Failed Apology

Enter Travis Kalanick, the man with the charisma of a cinder block. His apologies were about as effective as chopsticks are to eating a bowl of soup. Let's take a look at one of his gems:

*"I need to fundamentally change as a leader and grow up. This is the first time I've been willing to admit that I need leadership help and I intend to get it. I want to profoundly apologize to [the driver] as well as the driver and rider community and to the Uber team."*

Wow, riveting stuff, Travis. He managed to make it all about himself, didn't he? "I need to change, I need help, I want to apologize." It's like watching a teenager sulk because they got caught sneaking out. Where's the accountability?

Where's the plan of action? This apology was less about fixing the problems and more about saving face. No wonder it flopped harder than a bad sitcom pilot.

## The Backlash

The public reaction? Let's just say it wasn't pretty. Employees were fed up, investors were furious, and the media had a field day. Hashtags like #DeleteUber trended as users jumped ship to Lyft in droves. The backlash wasn't just digital—Uber faced protests and legal battles, too. The company's reputation was dragged through the mud, and rightly so. Kalanick's hollow words did nothing to stem the tide of public outrage. Instead, they fueled it. The general consensus? Uber was all talk and no action, and people were done giving them the benefit of the doubt.

## How It Could Have Been Done Better

So, what would a great apology have looked like?

*To all our employees, drivers, riders, and the public, I am deeply sorry for the toxic culture and unethical practices that have come to light at Uber. Our company has failed to uphold the values we claim to stand for, and for that, I take full responsibility. Effective immediately, we are implementing a zero-tolerance policy for harassment and discrimination, and we will be conducting a thorough, independent investigation into our practices.*

*We are committed to making Uber a safe, respectful, and ethical workplace. This means overhauling our leadership, providing mandatory training for all employees, and establishing clear, enforceable guidelines to prevent future misconduct. We are also setting up a fund to support our drivers and employees who have been affected by our past failures.*

*Actions speak louder than words, and you will see these changes take effect immediately. I understand that rebuilding trust will take time, but I am committed to earning back the respect of our community through tangible actions and transparency. Thank you for holding us accountable.*

There you go. Acknowledgment of the issues, a clear plan of action, and a commitment to change. Throw in some real restitution, like financial support for affected employees and drivers, and you've got yourself a decent start at mending fences. If Uber had taken this route, maybe—just maybe—they wouldn't have been the poster child for corporate dysfunction in 2017.

# 11

# Oops, I Did It Again: The Art of Repeat Apologies

You might think, "Okay, Dr. Jon, I've got this. I'll apologize once, and everything will be good, right?" Not so fast. When you screw up big time, don't expect a single "sorry" to magically fix everything. Some hurts are like that terrible song stuck in your head—they keep coming back. Some emotional wounds need more than just a quick fix. They require consistent, repeated acknowledgment of the pain you caused.

Let's be real, sometimes the damage is like trying to clean up glitter—one sweep doesn't do it. Each time you apologize, you're getting a little more of that mess cleaned up. So, if you find yourself saying "sorry" again and again, don't whine about it. Embrace it as the necessary consequence of your actions. Your partner needs to hear it multiple times to start believing you actually mean it. Not everyone processes trauma this way, but some do, and embracing it is easier than fighting it.

## The Right Attitude: Patience and Grace

Think of it like planting a garden. You don't just throw seeds on the ground and expect a lush landscape overnight. You water, you weed, you wait. The same goes for apologies. Your partner needs time to process their feelings, and your job is to be there, consistently showing that you care and that you're genuinely remorseful. Impatience screams insincerity, and trust me, your partner can smell that a mile away.

Nobody likes apologizing. It's uncomfortable, humbling, and often downright embarrassing. But if you want to make things right, you need to do it with grace. That means no eye-rolling, no huffing, and definitely no "I already said I'm sorry, what more do you want?" Grace in apologies means showing humility and understanding, even when you feel like you've apologized a million times already.

Grace is about putting your partner's feelings above your own ego. It's about recognizing their pain is valid and your job is to help heal it, not defend yourself. When you apologize with grace, you show you're not just in it for yourself but genuinely care about making things right. It's the difference between a hollow "sorry" and a heartfelt one.

## Recognizing When an Apology Needs to Be Revisited

So, you thought your apology was a slam dunk, but things are still icy at home? That's a clear sign your initial apology didn't cut it. Maybe your partner nodded and said it was fine, but their body language screamed otherwise. If you're still getting the cold shoulder or passive-aggressive comments, it's time to face the music: your apology wasn't enough - even if you did do everything right.

Look out for those subtle (and not-so-subtle) signs. Silence, avoidance, or even outright anger can indicate that your first attempt missed the mark. Instead of patting yourself on the back for trying, dig deeper. Ask your partner what's still bothering them and be prepared to listen without getting defensive. Remember, the goal is to heal, not to win.

Certain triggers can yank old wounds right back to the surface. It could be a place, a phrase, or even a seemingly unrelated event that reminds them of your past screw-up. And guess what? It's your job to understand these triggers and address them head-on. When you see your partner getting upset over something that reminds them of your past mistake, acknowledge it. Revisit your apology, reaffirm your commitment to change, and show that you're aware of the ongoing impact of your actions.

## Balancing Apologies with Actions

Words are just hot air without actions to back them up. If you want your apologies to mean anything, you've got to show through your behavior that you're genuinely committed to change. This isn't rocket science. If you keep doing the same thing that hurt your partner, your apologies are worthless.

Start by identifying the behaviors that caused the pain and make a conscious effort to change them. This might mean breaking bad habits, being more mindful, or making concrete commitments to improve. It's about walking the walk, not just talking the talk. Your partner needs to see consistent actions that align with your words. Only then will your apologies start to rebuild trust.

Consistency is key. One grand gesture isn't going to fix everything if you go back to your old ways the next day. Your partner is watching to see if your actions match your apologies over the long haul. They need to see that your commitment to change isn't just a flash in the pan but a sustained effort.

Make small, everyday changes that show you're serious about making things right. Whether it's being more attentive, following through on promises, or simply being kinder and more considerate, these consistent actions reinforce your apologies. They show you're not just sorry in the moment but are dedicated to being better in the future. Consistency builds credibility and trust.

## Dealing with Apology Fatigue

So, you've been spitting out apologies like a malfunctioning Pez dispenser, and now your partner looks ready to strangle you with those insincere "sorry"s. Welcome to apology fatigue, where your half-baked apologies are about as welcome as a fart in an elevator. If your partner rolls their eyes every time you mutter "sorry," it's a clear sign you've hit rock bottom in the apology department.

Take a hard look at why your apologies are about as effective as a helmet for a kamikaze pilot. Are you screwing up the same way over and over? Stop using apologies as a band-aid for your repeat offenses. Your partner doesn't need another empty "sorry"; they need you to fix your crap. Show them you're serious about change, not just spewing more empty words.

To dodge apology fatigue, you've got to change the game. Mix up your approach. Write a genuine note, plan a meaningful gesture, or sit down for a no-BS conversation about how you're going to stop being a screw-up. Show your partner that you're evolving, not just recycling the same old apologies.

Be proactive for once. Instead of waiting for your partner to call you out, own up to your mistakes first. Demonstrate what you're doing to ensure you don't mess up again. This shows you're not just apologizing to shut them up but because you actually care about fixing things. Proactive apologies can break the monotony and prove you're taking their feelings seriously.

## Apologizing for Chronic Issues

Alright, let's cut to the chase: if you keep screwing up in the same way, your apologies are about as effective as charging your electric car with a cell phone battery. Chronic issues require more than just a "sorry." They demand a serious look at your behavior patterns. You need to figure out why you keep making the same mistakes and address the root cause. This isn't just about apologizing; it's about committing to real, lasting change.

Start by identifying the behaviors that are causing the problem. Are you always late? Do you have a habit of making snarky comments? Whatever it is, recognize it and own up to it. Then, make a plan to change it. Apologies for chronic issues mean nothing if you're not actively working to fix the underlying behavior. Show your partner you're serious by taking concrete steps to change.

If you're stuck in a loop of screwing up and apologizing, it's time to break the cycle. This isn't a hamster wheel you want to be on. First, get some self-awareness. Pay attention to the triggers and situations that lead to your repeated mistakes. Understanding why you keep messing up is the first step to stopping it.

Next, take proactive steps to avoid these pitfalls. If you know you get cranky when you're hungry, keep a snack handy. If you lash out when stressed, find healthier ways to cope. The goal is to prevent the need for repeated apologies by addressing the issues head-on. This shows your partner you're not just sorry for the past but committed to a better future.

Self-awareness is like the GPS for your personal growth journey. Without it, you're just wandering aimlessly, repeating the same mistakes. If you want to stop apologizing for the same crap over and over, you need to get a handle on your own behavior. Take a hard look at yourself and be honest about your flaws. This isn't about beating yourself up; it's about understanding where you need to improve.

Once you've got a grip on your issues, focus on self-improvement. Read books, take courses, get therapy—do whatever it takes to become a better version of yourself. Self-awareness paired with a genuine desire to improve shows your partner you're committed to change. It's not just about saying "sorry" anymore; it's about proving through your actions you're serious about becoming a better person.

## The Impact of Repeated Apologies on the Apologizer

Repeated apologies can be a mirror reflecting back your own flaws. It's not fun to look into that mirror and see the same mistakes staring back at you, but it's a necessary step for personal growth. Each time you apologize, you're given an opportunity to self-reflect and understand why you keep messing up. It's like a never-ending feedback loop, forcing you to confront your shortcomings.

Use this as a chance to grow. Instead of wallowing in guilt, see it as a push to become a better person. Embrace the discomfort and let it drive you to make meaningful changes. Repeated apologies can be a catalyst for self-improvement, helping you to become more self-aware and empathetic. It's a painful process, but ultimately, it's one that can lead to significant personal growth.

While it's important to take responsibility for your actions, drowning in self-blame and guilt isn't going to help anyone. It's easy to spiral into a pit of self-loathing when you find yourself apologizing over and over. But wallowing in guilt is just another way to make it all about you, instead of focusing on the person you've hurt.

Acknowledge your mistakes, yes. But don't let guilt paralyze you. Instead, use it as motivation to change. Remember, the goal is to repair the relationship and improve yourself, not to beat yourself up endlessly. Self-blame can be as toxic as the actions that led to your apologies in the first place. Focus on constructive change rather than destructive self-criticism.

Every apology is a lesson if you're paying attention. The process of repeatedly apologizing forces you to learn and evolve. It's like an unrelenting school of hard knocks, but the tuition is worth it. Each time you say "sorry," you're given a chance to understand your partner better and to make adjustments in your behavior.

Take these lessons to heart. Reflect on what each apology teaches you about your actions and your partner's needs. Use this knowledge to evolve. The goal isn't just to apologize better, but to become someone who doesn't need to apologize as much. Let the process of repeated apologies shape you into a more understanding, empathetic, and self-aware person. It's not just about mending the relationship; it's about becoming a better you.

## Handling Rejection of Repeated Apologies

So, you've been apologizing like your life depends on it, and your partner still isn't forgiving you. That stings. But guess what? You can't force forgiveness. Sometimes, despite your best efforts, your partner isn't ready to let go of their hurt. It's a tough pill to swallow, but it's part of the process. Coping with a lack of forgiveness means acknowledging their feelings and giving them the space they need.

It's crucial to remember their forgiveness isn't a given, no matter how sincere your apologies are. Focus on being patient and understanding. Keep showing you're committed to change, even if they're not ready to accept your apologies right now. It's about respecting their healing process and continuing to demonstrate your remorse through your actions.

Not every apology will be accepted, and that's something you'll have to come to terms with. People are complicated, and so are their emotions. Your partner might be dealing with their own internal struggles that make forgiveness difficult. It's not always a reflection of your apology's sincerity but rather their capacity to move past the hurt at this time.

Accepting that your apology might not be accepted is part of the growth process. It doesn't mean you stop trying, but it does mean you manage your expectations. Keep showing up, keep improving, and understand forgiveness is a journey, not a destination. Sometimes, the best you can do is to keep being consistent in your efforts and hope that, with time, your partner will come around.

Rejection of your apology isn't the end of the road. It's a detour, not a dead end. Moving forward after rejection means continuing to show you're committed to change, regardless of immediate forgiveness. It's about proving through your actions you're sincere, even if your partner isn't ready to acknowledge it yet.

Keep focusing on self-improvement and consistent positive behavior. Don't let the rejection deter you from doing the right thing. Use it as motivation to keep striving for better. Remember, rebuilding trust takes time, and even if your partner isn't ready to forgive now, your continued efforts can eventually make a difference. Stay patient, stay committed, and keep moving forward, one step at a time.

## As Many Times as it Takes

I get it—apologizing over and over sucks, especially when you know you screwed up. It's like a never-ending cycle of guilt and exhaustion, and you start thinking, "Is this relationship ever going to be okay again?" It's a trap, and the more you flail around trying to escape, the tighter those ropes get. You end up feeling even more stuck, and your will to fix things evaporates faster than a beer at a frat party. The trick is finding that zen-like stillness, accepting your screw-up, and doing what's necessary to mend things. Now, let me tell you about Rachel and Joseph, a couple who stumbled into my office and learned that repeating a genuine apology was the missing piece in their healing puzzle.

Rachel and Joseph walked into my office like many couples before them, carrying the invisible weight of years of unresolved conflict and unspoken pain. Rachel, a round-faced woman with soft eyes that seemed perpetually tired, moved with the careful grace of someone who had learned to carry emotional burdens as if they were physical. She wore a loose, comfortable sweater and practical shoes, the kind of clothes that spoke of a life focused more on surviving than thriving. Beside her, Joseph loomed large, his tall, thick frame and booming voice giving him the presence of a gentle giant who seemed bewildered by the intricacies of his own marriage.

As they took their seats on the plush blue couch, I could sense the tension between them, a palpable thing that seemed to fill the room. Rachel's hands fidgeted with the hem of her sweater, her eyes darting from Joseph to me, as if searching for an anchor in a storm. Joseph, on the other hand, sat with his shoulders hunched and his hands resting awkwardly on his knees, his face a mixture of frustration and helplessness. Despite his imposing size, there was a vulnerability in his eyes, a silent plea for understanding that belied his outward confidence.

Their story began not with the usual pleasantries, but with Rachel's trembling voice breaking the silence. "You have no idea how many times he's caused trauma in my life, Dr. Jon," she said, her words heavy with the weight of years of neglect and unhealed wounds. It was clear from the start that this was a couple on the brink, their marriage a fragile thing held together by the thinnest of threads. Yet, beneath the layers of resentment and hurt, there was still a flicker of something—perhaps hope, perhaps love—that had brought them to my office seeking a way forward.

Rachel's words spilled out like a dam bursting. "You ruined my last meal with my mother."

Joseph shifted uncomfortably, his voice rising despite his effort to keep it calm. "Rachel, that happened twelve years ago. Twelve. Years."

She shot him a look, her frustration palpable. "For twelve years, you've been trying to sweep it under the rug."

He ran a hand through his hair, a gesture of helplessness. "I've apologized for it dozens of times."

"Your apologies are always dismissive," she snapped back, her voice cracking.

I raised a hand, signaling for them to pause. "Rachel, please, tell me the whole story. Joseph, I need you to listen without interrupting."

Rachel took a deep breath, her shoulders dropping slightly as if the weight of the memory was already pressing down on her. "Thank you, Dr. Jon," she said, her voice softer now. "I would love to tell you the story."

She began to recount the night with a mix of melancholy and anger. "My mother was sick, dying of cancer. She had been bedridden for months, but one evening she had a burst of energy. From her hospice bed, she said she wanted to go out one last time for dinner with us. Joseph refused to cancel his plans with a business colleague. We were new in town, and both kids were under three. I couldn't leave them alone, so I missed the last dinner I could have had with my mother. She passed away a week later."

The room fell silent, the weight of her words hanging in the air. Joseph sighed deeply, his head bowed. "I've apologized for that. I don't know how we're supposed to move forward if you keep holding this over my head."

"How many times do you think you've apologized for it?" I asked him, my tone gentle but firm.

"At least ten times," he muttered, his voice barely above a whisper.

Rachel rolled her eyes, her frustration bubbling to the surface. "That's a gross exaggeration."

I turned to Rachel. "How many times has he apologized in a way where you felt he truly regretted it?"

She paused, thinking back. "Once, towards my mother's funeral. The rest felt like I was pushing him."

I looked at Joseph, seeing the genuine remorse in his eyes. "Do you truly regret it?"

His voice broke slightly as he replied, "Of all the things I regret, it's the biggest one."

"Rachel," I said softly, "I need you to stop and appreciate what he just said."

She blinked, her eyes moistening.

I then turned to Joseph. "It was a big mistake, and you have to apologize for it any time she brings it up. She's not doing it to punish you; she's struggling to process it. She wants to believe that nothing like this will ever happen again. So, you have to apologize and let the apology hang there until she feels satisfied."

Joseph nodded, his face earnest. He turned to Rachel. "I am so sorry for that night. I wish I could go back and change it. I regret it every day."

Rachel's eyes filled with tears. "Thank you... that makes the second time I believe you were actually sorry."

The room was filled with a sense of release, the heavy burden of unspoken pain and guilt finally starting to lift.

This session marked the beginning of a new chapter for Rachel and Joseph. For the first time, Joseph seemed to grasp the depth of Rachel's hurt and the significance of a heartfelt apology. His understanding that apologies were not just about uttering words, but about acknowledging her pain and helping her heal, signaled a pivotal change. It was clear that this wouldn't be the last time Joseph would need to apologize, but he now had a newfound confidence and energy to offer genuine apologies that could aid Rachel's healing process.

Rachel's outburst, followed by her tearful acknowledgment of Joseph's remorse, was a crucial breakthrough. It highlighted the importance of a sincere apology in mending broken trust and healing old wounds. Her emotional response indicated that she felt heard and validated, which was essential for rebuilding their connection. This moment of genuine remorse from Joseph allowed her to begin the process of letting go of some of the long-held pain.

Moving forward, the real challenge for Joseph would be to maintain this level of empathy and understanding. Every time Rachel brought up the painful memory, it was an opportunity for him to reinforce his commitment to change and to reassure her that such neglect would not happen again. This understanding created a new dynamic in their relationship, where Rachel could begin to trust that her feelings mattered and that Joseph was committed to being the partner she needed.

## Celebrating Progress and Healing

Amidst all the apologizing and self-reflection, it's easy to forget to celebrate the wins, no matter how small. When you and your partner start to see improvements, take a moment to acknowledge them. Maybe they're not rolling their eyes as much, or perhaps they've started to open up more. These small signs are progress. Recognize them and celebrate them together.

Acknowledging improvements isn't just about patting yourself on the back. It's about reinforcing the positive changes and showing your partner you notice and appreciate their efforts too. A simple "I've noticed we're arguing less, and I really appreciate it" can go a long way. It reinforces the progress and builds a positive feedback loop that encourages further healing and growth.

You've been working hard, and it's starting to pay off. When you hit significant milestones—like your partner expressing forgiveness or showing signs of renewed trust—celebrate them. These moments are critical in the journey of healing. They're not just checkpoints but validations of all the hard work and effort you've both put in.

Plan a special date, write a heartfelt note, or simply take a moment to express your gratitude and joy. Celebrating these milestones helps solidify them, making them more than just fleeting moments. It's a way of marking the progress you've made and setting a positive tone for the future. Don't let these moments slip by unnoticed; they're the building blocks of a stronger, healthier relationship.

Healing is a long road, and maintaining a positive outlook is crucial. It's easy to get bogged down by past mistakes and ongoing challenges, but focusing on the progress and the potential for the future can keep you motivated. Foster an optimistic outlook by regularly discussing your goals and dreams as a couple. Talk about the future you're working towards and the steps you're taking to get there.

Keep the focus on the positive changes and the strength you're building together. This doesn't mean ignoring the issues that still need work, but rather balancing them with a hopeful perspective. By fostering a positive outlook, you're not just surviving the tough times; you're actively building a brighter future together. Celebrate your progress and keep your eyes on the horizon. The journey may be challenging, but the destination is worth it.

# Apology Hall of Shame: Volkswagen Emissions 2015

In the world of corporate screw-ups, Volkswagen's 2015 emissions scandal is a goldmine of failure. The company got caught with their hands in the pollution jar, cheating on emissions tests for their diesel engines. The scandal perfectly illustrates the need for multiple apologies when you've really screwed up. VW's half-hearted attempts at saying "sorry" were so bad they could serve as textbook examples of what not to do.

### The Incident

In September 2015, the U.S. Environmental Protection Agency (EPA) dropped a bombshell: Volkswagen had installed software in their diesel cars to cheat on emissions tests. This "defeat device" would detect when the car was being tested and reduce emissions accordingly. On the road, however, these cars spewed nitrogen oxides at up to 40 times the legal limit. This wasn't just a handful of cars either—about 11 million vehicles worldwide were affected.

The deception wasn't just some rogue engineer's brainchild. It turned out to be a widespread, systematic effort involving high-level executives. In other words, this wasn't just a simple mistake—it was a full-blown corporate conspiracy to lie and pollute. In other words, business as usual for corporate corruption.

### The Failed Apology

Volkswagen's initial response was almost as bad as the scandal itself. Martin Winterkorn, the CEO at the time, issued a vague, wishy-washy apology that lacked any real substance. Here it is, in all its limp glory:

*"I personally am deeply sorry that we have broken the trust of our customers and the public. We will cooperate fully with the responsible agencies with transparency*

*and urgency to clearly, openly, and completely establish all of the facts of this case. Volkswagen has ordered an external investigation of this matter. "*

This apology failed on multiple fronts. First, it was impersonal and lacked specifics. Winterkorn didn't even mention the cheating directly. It was as if he was sorry for some minor customer service mishap, not a global environmental scandal. Second, the promise of an external investigation came off as a hollow gesture—everyone knew VW had been caught red-handed.

## The Backlash

The public and media response to VW's apology was swift and brutal. Consumers felt betrayed, environmentalists were outraged, and regulators were furious. Social media exploded with anger and mockery. Hashtags like #dieselgate and #VWGate trended for weeks. The company's stock price plummeted, and they faced billions in fines and lawsuits.

By now you should see a pattern in this section of the book - bad apologies cost companies billions of dollars. If that's not enough motivation to learn how to do this right I really don't know what to say to convince you to take the time to learn this powerful skill.

Adding fuel to the fire, VW's apology was seen as evasive. It failed to address the core issue: Volkswagen's deliberate, calculated effort to deceive regulators and the public. Instead of taking full responsibility, VW's apology came off as a corporate PR stunt designed to minimize damage.

## How the Apology Could Have Been Better

Volkswagen's apology needed a major overhaul. They should have acknowledged their wrongdoing explicitly, making it clear that the company deliberately cheated emissions tests to make their cars appear more environmentally friendly. Taking full responsibility was crucial; VW needed to accept the deception was entirely their fault without trying to shift blame. Providing specifics and transparency by fully cooperating with investigations and making findings public would have helped.

Offering concrete actions and restitution, such as recalling affected vehicles, providing free repairs, and investing in green technologies and environmental remediation, would have shown a genuine commitment to making amends. Finally, they needed to apologize sincerely and repeatedly, showing genuine remorse for the harm caused and communicating openly to regain trust.

Here's what a decent apology from Volkswagen might have sounded like:

*We at Volkswagen are deeply ashamed of our actions. We deliberately installed software to cheat emissions tests, deceiving regulators and the public. This was not a mistake but a conscious decision, and we accept full responsibility. We are recalling all affected vehicles and providing free repairs. We will invest a substantial amount of capital in green technologies to offset the damage we've caused. We promise to cooperate fully with all investigations and make our findings public. We are truly sorry for betraying your trust and harming the environment. We will work tirelessly to regain your trust and ensure this never happens again.*

Had VW issued a sincere, detailed apology like this and followed through with concrete actions, they might have mitigated some of the damage. Instead, their vague, evasive apologies only deepened the public's distrust and anger.

# 12

# Wait, What About My Apology?

So, you've been slogging through this book, nodding your head, and muttering to yourself, "Yep, that's my partner all right." If you're still here, there's a better than 50% chance you're not the one who needs to apologize better. Nope, the real culprit is probably sitting next to you, blissfully unaware of their own apology deficit. Welcome to the club.

## When Your Partner is the Apology Avoider

Let's dive into the murky waters of relationships where one partner just can't seem to find the magic words: "I'm sorry." Maybe your relationship feels like it's stuck in a swamp of unresolved issues, resentment growing like mold in a forgotten Tupperware. You're not alone. The inability to apologize is like a wrecking ball to your relationship. Every unacknowledged mistake chips away at the trust, love, and respect you've built together.

Think about the last fight you had. Remember the silent treatment, the passive-aggressive comments, the nights spent staring at opposite walls in bed? That's the fallout of an unspoken apology. It's like being forced to eat a bland, overcooked steak every night—disappointing, frustrating, and ultimately unsatisfying.

Don't worry, though. We're about to arm you with the tools to extract an apology from your partner without resorting to waterboarding. We're going to explore a few techniques to help you get that elusive "I'm sorry" out of them. Think of it as an excavation project—you're digging for emotional gold in the rocky terrain of their stubbornness.

## Trading Apologies: The Diplomatic Approach

First up, let's talk about trading apologies. This is like a diplomatic negotiation where both sides concede a little to gain a lot. Here's how to do it without making them feel like they're signing a surrender treaty.

Start by acknowledging that both of you might have some apologizing to do. This isn't just about them, even if you're 99% sure they're the primary offender. By positioning it as a mutual exchange, you lower their defenses and make the idea of apologizing less daunting.

You should apologize first. Yes, you read that right. I know, it sounds like eating a soggy salad while they get the steak, but trust me on this one. When you take the lead in apologizing, you set the tone for the entire exchange. A heartfelt, detailed, and sincere apology from you demonstrates the level of effort and emotion you expect in return. If you go in half-hearted, don't be surprised when you get the same lackluster response from them. By showing them how it's done, you're creating a standard for what a proper apology should look like.

Leading by example also shows maturity and a genuine desire to mend the relationship. It takes guts to be the first to apologize, especially when you feel wronged. However, this act of vulnerability can encourage your partner to let down their guard and reflect on their actions. When they see your sincere effort, it can inspire them to reciprocate with equal honesty and remorse. Setting this precedent can transform the dynamic of your relationship, making both of you more willing to take responsibility and communicate openly.

Your apology should serve as a template for theirs. Be specific about what you're apologizing for, express genuine remorse, and explain how you'll avoid the same mistake in the future. This approach gives them a clear roadmap to follow when it's their turn. Think of it as teaching them how to dance: you lead, they follow, and eventually, you're in sync. By laying out your apology clearly, you help them understand the components of a sincere and effective apology, making it easier for them to mirror your approach.

This method not only helps your partner see what a good apology looks like but also fosters a culture of accountability in your relationship. When both partners understand the importance of specificity, remorse, and commitment to change, it sets a foundation for healthier interactions. By modeling the perfect apology, you're not just seeking resolution for the current issue; you're also equipping your partner with the tools to handle future conflicts more constructively. This mutual understanding can lead to a stronger, more resilient relationship where both parties feel heard and valued.

**Asking for an Apology After a Delay**

Sometimes, the best way to get an apology isn't in the heat of the moment. You need to let things cool off first. Think of it like cooking a steak—if you keep poking it, it's never going to cook right. Let it rest, and it'll be so much better. Here's how to master the art of delayed apologies.

First things first, you need to give it some time. If you go in demanding an apology right after a fight, you're likely to get a defensive, half-assed "sorry" that's about as sincere as a televangelist saying they can heal your cancer. Immediate apologies are often filled with resentment and defensiveness. By waiting, you allow both of you to cool down and gain perspective. This isn't about letting them off the hook; it's about creating the right conditions for a meaningful apology.

Letting things settle gives your partner time to reflect on their actions without feeling pressured. It also gives you time to process your feelings and approach the conversation with a clear head. This cooling-off period is crucial because it turns a potential shouting match into a constructive dialogue. Patience is your ally here. Remember, you're playing the long game for a sincere apology and a stronger relationship.

## Jot Down Your Grievances

While you're waiting for the emotional storm to pass, do yourself a favor and write down what bothered you. Get specific. Think of it as your personal burn book, but less Regina George and more self-help. Write down exactly what they did that upset you and the ideal apology you wanted to hear. This exercise helps you clarify your thoughts and ensures you don't forget important details when it's time to have that conversation.

Writing things down also serves another purpose: it prevents you from exaggerating the incident in your mind. Often, our memories of conflicts become distorted over time. By documenting your feelings and what happened, you create an accurate account that you can reference later. Plus, having your ideal apology written out gives you a clear picture of what you need to hear to feel better. It's like preparing a script for the emotional resolution you're aiming for.

## Timing is Everything

Now, here's the tricky part—finding the right moment to bring it up. You don't want to do it when either of you is still fuming. Wait for a time when you're both happy and relaxed. Maybe you're having a nice dinner, or you've just had a good laugh together. Happiness is your secret weapon here. People are more receptive when they're in a good mood. Catching your partner at the right time can make all the difference.

Timing your conversation during a positive moment also shows your partner that you value the relationship and are committed to resolving issues without causing further tension. It's like planting seeds in fertile soil—they're much more likely to grow. This approach sets a constructive tone for the conversation and increases the chances that your partner will be open and responsive to what you have to say.

### Lay the Foundation with Love

When you've found your moment, start by professing your love and your desire to have a great relationship. Yes, it sounds a bit mushy, but it works. Tell your partner how much they mean to you and how you want to make things even better between you two. By expressing your love first, you soften the blow and make it clear that your request for an apology comes from a place of wanting to improve the relationship, not to blame or shame.

This approach not only shows vulnerability but also emphasizes that you're a team. It's not you versus them; it's both of you working together to make things right. Gently segue into the fact that you're still holding on to some resentment. Make it clear that this isn't an attack, but rather a way for both of you to grow closer. Your honesty can pave the way for a more open and understanding dialogue.

### The Soft Sell Approach

Explain that their apology would mean a lot to you and help you move past your resentment. Be honest about your feelings but avoid sounding accusatory. Something like, "I love you, and our relationship means everything to me. I've been holding onto some hurt from our last argument, and I think if we could talk about it, it would help me move on. Your acknowledgment of how I feel would mean a lot." This phrasing highlights your emotional needs without placing blame.

By using this approach, you're setting the stage for a heartfelt apology. You're showing vulnerability and opening the door for your partner to step up and show they care. Remember, it's not just about getting an apology; it's about fostering understanding and strengthening your relationship. By making it clear that their apology can help you heal, you encourage them to take responsibility

for their actions and contribute to the emotional well-being of your relationship.

## Ask for It in Writing

Sometimes, asking for an apology face-to-face feels like volunteering for a root
canal. The good news is that 90% of our communication is non-verbal. This
also means that 90% of the fear of confrontation comes from those non-verbal
cues—eye rolls, sighs, and that infuriating look of confusion that makes you
want to throw something. Solution? Write it down. A text or email strips
away the fear factor, making it easier for them to digest. It's like serving a bitter
pill with a spoonful of sugar. Plus, they can't interrupt you with defensive
nonsense.

The beauty of written communication is that it lets you lay out your
thoughts clearly and calmly, without the risk of an immediate emotional
explosion. When you write down your request for an apology, you have the
chance to be precise and thorough. This method also gives your partner time
to reflect on your words without feeling cornered. So, grab your phone or
laptop and channel your inner Shakespeare—or Dr. Phil, whichever works.

The more detail you provide about why you need the apology, the better.
Explain if it's preventing you from growing in the relationship. Maybe it's a
piece of resentment that's festering like an old, forgotten sandwich in the back
of the fridge. Or perhaps it's making you cold and distant, turning your once
warm and fuzzy relationship into the emotional equivalent of Siberia. Be
specific. If you're trying to change something fundamental, like affection or
behavior, lay it out there. Don't be vague; vagueness is the enemy of progress.

Think of your message as a mini-novel of grievances. Your partner needs
to understand the depth of your feelings and the impact their actions (or
lack of apologies) are having on you. Detail why this apology is crucial for
moving forward. Highlight how it's affecting your daily interactions and
overall happiness. Paint a vivid picture—they need to see the full technicolor
version of your pain, not just the black-and-white outline.

And while you're at it, make sure to specify if you're okay with receiving the apology in writing or if you need it in person. If you don't, they'll respond in written form or, worse, with silence 100% of the time. It's like leaving the door wide open for them to chicken out. If an in-person apology is essential for you to feel closure, say so. Otherwise, expect a text that reads, "sry" and nothing else. Or the deafening sound of silence, which is even worse.

Clarifying your preference helps avoid misunderstandings and ensures you get the type of apology that will actually help you heal. If written apologies feel too impersonal, emphasize the need for a face-to-face conversation. This clarity can prevent further frustration and shows your partner that you're serious about resolving the issue properly. You're not just after words; you're after meaningful, heartfelt words delivered in a way that resonates with you.

Lastly, it's crucial to set a time limit for their response and follow up or check in with your partner. Without a deadline, your request will get swept under the rug faster than dust bunnies in a spring cleaning frenzy. Accountability is key. Give them a reasonable but firm deadline. Think of it as a polite nudge rather than a court summons.

Following up isn't about nagging; it's about ensuring that your needs are taken seriously. A simple, "Hey, did you get a chance to think about what I wrote?" can keep the conversation moving. If they're dragging their feet, remind them gently but firmly. You're not letting this slide into the abyss of forgotten promises. You deserve closure, and that means keeping the pressure on—just enough to make sure they follow through without feeling harassed.

In the end, asking for an apology in writing can be a game-changer. It reduces the immediate stress of confrontation, allows you to articulate your feelings clearly, and sets the stage for a thoughtful response. Just remember to be detailed, set your terms, and enforce accountability. With these steps, you're well on your way to getting that much-needed apology and moving forward in your relationship.

## Tell Them What You Need to Hear

When it comes to asking for an apology, telling your partner exactly what you need to hear can make all the difference. Let's face it, expecting them to magically know what to say is like expecting a cat to understand quantum physics—it's not happening. You can reference this book and, if they're open to it, give it to them as a gift. Nothing says "I love you, please stop screwing up" like a thoughtful present that doubles as a relationship manual. Handing over this book can be your subtle, yet effective way of saying, "Here, read this and learn how not to be a jerk."

Gifting them this book serves multiple purposes. It shows you're invested in improving the relationship and gives them a concrete resource to understand what you need. It's not just about demanding an apology; it's about equipping them with the knowledge to do it right. This approach can take the pressure off you to explain everything and allows them to see things from your perspective through an objective source. Plus, it's a gift that keeps on giving—every chapter is a goldmine of insights for better communication.

You can use the bullet points laid out in this book to help make their apology meaningful. I recommend focusing on three components: understanding what hurt you, expressing remorse, and committing to change that behavior moving forward. These are the most important elements. While it would be nice to get everything, it's not always possible, so lower the bar for success if you can. Setting realistic expectations helps prevent disappointment and encourages genuine effort from your partner. If they nail these three aspects, consider it a win.

Break it down for them: Understanding what hurt you means they need to acknowledge the specific actions or words that caused pain. Expressing remorse involves them showing genuine regret for their actions, not just mouthing the words "I'm sorry." And committing to change means they have to outline concrete steps they will take to avoid repeating the same mistakes. By focusing on these three components, you provide a clear, achievable roadmap for their apology. It's like giving them a cheat sheet for emotional success.

The more parts of the process you can handle for your partner, the better. If you can do the work we talked about in Chapter 7, where you explain all the ways in which you were hurt so they don't have to pull it out of you, that would be great. It's like handing them a fully loaded GPS with the destination already programmed in. They don't have to guess or get lost; they just have to follow the directions. This proactive approach not only makes it easier for them to apologize but also ensures that you feel fully heard and understood.

Think of it as setting them up for a slam dunk. When you provide them with all the details of how you were hurt, you eliminate the guesswork and make it straightforward for them to address your pain points. This can reduce their anxiety about apologizing and increase the likelihood of a sincere, effective apology. Plus, it shows that you're committed to resolving the issue constructively, rather than waiting for them to stumble through it on their own.

By guiding your partner through what you need to hear, you're not just facilitating an apology—you're teaching them how to communicate better and fostering a deeper understanding between you two. This isn't about making them grovel; it's about creating a space where both of you can express your feelings openly and honestly. With these steps, you'll be well on your way to receiving the meaningful apology you deserve and building a stronger, more resilient relationship.

## Accepting a Non-Apology

Learning to read non-apologies from your partner is like decoding a secret language. Take my wife, for instance. She's not a fan of apologizing. Despite tremendous growth in this area during our marriage, she still finds it really hard to say the words. In our marriage, if she gets distant for a while and then sidles up next to me on the couch, gently placing her head on my shoulder, I've learned to accept that as her version of an apology 80% of the time.

It's her way of saying, "I don't want to fight anymore, can we move on?" without actually having to say it. There are those other times when I really need her to verbalize it, and I will ask, but I've also come to accept that I just won't get a verbal apology every time. So, I look for that head-on-shoulder moment and take it as a sign she wants peace.

Understanding these non-verbal cues has been a game-changer in our relationship. It's about recognizing that sometimes actions speak louder than words. When she leans in and rests her head on my shoulder, it's her way of bridging the gap. I've learned to appreciate these gestures as genuine attempts to reconnect. Sure, I would love a clear-cut "I'm sorry" every time, but in reality, those head-on-shoulder moments carry their own weight and significance. Accepting these non-apologies requires a bit of flexibility and a lot of empathy. It's about understanding your partner's unique way of expressing remorse and being okay with it.

Learning to recognize the signs that your partner wants to move forward can make a huge difference. It's like having a cheat sheet for relationship peacekeeping. See if those signs are enough for you. Examples of non-apology signs include when they start talking to other family members about how they're upset that you're fighting. This might seem indirect, but it often indicates they're bothered by the conflict and want it resolved. Similarly, if they suddenly start doing chores or housework they normally avoid, it might be their way of making amends without saying the words.

Another classic sign is increased physical affection. If your partner gets more touchy-feely or clingy, it's usually a sign they regret the fight and are trying to show they still care. These gestures can be subtle yet powerful indicators of their desire to move past the conflict. Accepting these non-verbal apologies depends on your willingness to see these actions for what they are—genuine attempts to mend the relationship. It's about interpreting these behaviors as expressions of regret and understanding that not everyone is comfortable with verbal apologies.

Understanding these cues requires paying attention to your partner's behavior patterns. Maybe they make your favorite meal unexpectedly, or they start sharing more about their day, seeking closeness. These actions are their way of reaching out and trying to restore harmony. It's essential to acknowledge these efforts and respond positively, reinforcing that you recognize and appreciate their attempts at reconciliation. By doing so, you create a more forgiving and understanding dynamic in your relationship.

In the end, learning to read and accept non-apologies is about flexibility and empathy. It's recognizing that not everyone expresses remorse in the same way. By understanding your partner's unique signals, you can navigate conflicts more effectively and build a stronger, more resilient relationship. It's about finding peace in the unspoken gestures and appreciating the effort behind them.

## Skipping the Apology and Changing the Behavior

Sometimes, you've got to face the harsh reality that waiting for an apology from your partner is like waiting for a unicorn to show up at your front door. It's time to skip the apology altogether and focus on what really matters: changing the behavior. When clients first step into my office, I always ask what their goals are. For couples work, this translates to "Is there anything in the relationship you want to see stopped or started?" Often, it's about wanting more affection or putting an end to the yelling. The key is to get specific about the behavior you need to see changed and discuss it separately from the apology. Let's dive into the nitty-gritty of how to make this work.

Picture this: You're in a session, and your partner is sitting across from you, looking as clueless as ever. Instead of banging your head against the wall waiting for them to say "I'm sorry," shift the focus. Spell out exactly what behaviors you want to see changed. Maybe you want them to stop acting like they're auditioning for a part in a horror movie every time they yell. Or perhaps you're tired of living with a human ice sculpture and want to see more physical affection. Be crystal clear. Vague requests like "be nicer" are about as useful as a zipper on t-shirt. You need to pinpoint specific actions they need to start or stop.

When you frame your desires around behavior instead of apologies, you're putting the ball in their court with actionable items. It's like giving them a to-do list for being a better partner. "Stop screaming like a banshee when things go wrong," or "Initiate a hug once in a while so I know you're not a robot." These are tangible, concrete changes they can work on. By detaching the behavior from the need for an apology, you take a massive step towards actual improvement instead of getting stuck in the blame game.

The main goal of an apology is to make sure whatever happened in the past does not happen again so the relationship can remain intact and warm moving forward. Now, if you're willing to be the bigger person and forgo the remorse, groveling, and expression of sorrow that usually come with an apology, you can shift the conversation to behavior modification. Essentially, you're saying, "I don't need to hear you grovel; I need you to change." It's like upgrading from a band-aid to actual stitches to fix the wound.

Imagine telling your partner, "I don't need you to tell me you're sorry for being a jerk last week. I need you to stop being a jerk moving forward. If you can do that you get a pass for last week." This approach can be liberating. It focuses on forward motion rather than rehashing the past. It's not about letting them off the hook; it's about steering the ship towards calmer waters. And let's be honest, some people are terrible at apologizing. Expecting them to deliver a heartfelt apology is like expecting a squirrel to bark. It's just not in their DNA. So, why waste time on the impossible?

By focusing on behavior change, you're prioritizing the health of the relationship over the satisfaction of hearing an apology. You're looking at the bigger picture. A successful relationship isn't built on perfect apologies but on consistent actions that show growth and commitment. When you lay out your expectations for behavior, you set a clear path for your partner to follow. It's about creating a roadmap for a better future together, one action at a time.

So next time you're about to pull your hair out waiting for an apology, take a deep breath and pivot. Focus on what needs to change moving forward. Spell out the behaviors you want to see, and set clear expectations. By doing this, you're not only sidestepping the frustration of waiting for an apology that may never come, but you're also paving the way for a healthier, happier relationship. And who knows? Once your partner starts changing their behavior, you might just get that apology after all—wrapped in actions that speak louder than words.

# Apology Hall of Shame: Nike's Labor Practices in the 1990s

In the grand tapestry of corporate screw-ups, Nike's labor practices in the 1990s stand out like a particularly ugly patch. This chapter is all about how sometimes, even when you've royally messed up, you can move forward without an apology. It's like spilling red wine on the carpet and just putting a plant over the stain. Nike's handling of their labor scandal is a masterclass in dodging an apology but still coming out on top.

### The Incident

Let's travel back to the 1990s, a time when grunge was in, the internet was new, and Nike was churning out sneakers in sweatshops. Reports started flooding in about horrendous working conditions in factories overseas—child labor, miserable wages, and unsafe environments. Picture workers toiling away for pennies in sweltering factories, producing those iconic Swoosh-branded shoes. The media had a field day with this, plastering images of exploited workers everywhere. Nike was in the hot seat, and everyone was waiting for them to step up, admit their wrongdoings, and issue a heartfelt apology.

### The Non-Apology

But instead of apologizing, Nike pulled a classic corporate sidestep. They didn't issue a public apology. Nope, not a single "sorry" was uttered. Instead, they launched into a series of initiatives aimed at improving labor practices and boosting transparency. Sure, they made changes—better wages, improved working conditions, monitoring systems—but where was the groveling? The public was left hanging, expecting at least a token apology. The lack of an apology was a bold move, almost like saying, "Yeah, we did that. Now, watch us fix it without ever saying we're sorry."

## The Backlash

Predictably, the backlash was fierce. Activists, consumers, and media outlets tore into Nike. Protesters rallied, celebrities denounced them, and people burned their sneakers in dramatic displays of outrage. It was a PR nightmare. The lack of an apology only fueled the fire, making Nike seem arrogant and indifferent to the suffering they had caused. Their silence on the apology front was like pouring gasoline on the already blazing inferno of public outrage. The expectation of a corporate mea culpa was palpable across all media channels, but Nike just kept their lips sealed.

## Moving On Without Saying "Sorry"

And yet, despite the public fury, Nike managed to pull through. How? By taking meaningful action. They revamped their labor practices, set up independent monitoring systems, and made significant strides in corporate responsibility. They didn't just talk the talk—they walked the walk. Nike's actions, over time, started to speak louder than the apology that never came. Consumers gradually shifted their focus from the scandal to Nike's innovative products and marketing genius. It turns out, sometimes doing the right thing can overshadow the lack of an "I'm sorry."

Even without a groveling apology, Nike was able to regain its stature and maintain its position as a leading global brand. Their commitment to reforming labor practices and ensuring better conditions for workers began to change public perception. The takeaway here is clear: while a heartfelt apology can work wonders, consistent actions and genuine improvements can also pave the way to redemption. Nike didn't just survive the scandal—they thrived, proving that sometimes, actions really do speak louder than words.

In the end, Nike's handling of their labor scandal in the 1990s shows that moving forward without an apology is possible. It's not always about the words you say; it's about the actions you take. And while we'd all love a nice, clean apology wrapped in a bow, sometimes the best way to clean up a mess is to just get to work and start scrubbing. Nike did just that, and they're still standing strong, proving that even in the Apology Hall of Shame, there are lessons to be learned and victories to be had.

# 13

# Apology Motivation: Is It About You or Them?

APOLOGIZING. THE THING WE all love to avoid but can't escape, like taxes or bad reality TV. You've probably found yourself in the hot seat, scrambling to say sorry for something you did or didn't do, and you may have wondered, "Why the hell am I even doing this?" Well, congratulations, you're not alone in your misery.

There are two main reasons people apologize: fear and love. And let's be real, most of us are cowards, so fear usually takes the lead. We're terrified of the relationship crashing and burning, of being left alone with our sad selves, or of being abandoned like last season's fashion.

Fear-based apologies are like bringing a plastic fork to a sword fight. They're quick, panicked, and completely ineffective in the long run. You say sorry because you're scared of the fallout, not because you actually give a damn about fixing what you broke. But hey, it keeps the peace for a while, right? If a fear-based apology is all you can offer and you follow the steps laid out in this book chances are it's going to still do quite a lot of good, and just following the steps can eventually transform it into the other type of apology - a love-based one.

Love-based apologies are the unicorns of the apology world. These are the mature, grown-up version of saying sorry. You apologize out of love because you recognize that maybe, just maybe, you're not perfect. Shocking, I know. You realize your partner is hurting, and instead of clutching onto your ego like a life raft, you sacrifice it. You admit you're wrong, and in doing so, you give your partner a bit of strength. You show them it's okay to be flawed, which is a hell of a lot more comforting than pretending you're a perfect little angel.

Get ready. We're about to explore these two motivations in excruciating detail. By the end of this chapter, you might even figure out which camp you belong to. Spoiler alert: it's probably the fear one.

## The Role of Fear in Apologizing

Let's get into the meat of it: fear-based apologies. These are the bread and butter of half-hearted sorries everywhere. When you're apologizing out of fear, it's like trying to patch up a leaky boat with chewing gum. It might hold for a minute, but you're still sinking, buddy.

First up, we have the fear of the relationship ending. You know that gut-wrenching, stomach-churning panic that hits when you realize you've really messed up? Yeah, that's the fear of losing your cushy spot on the relationship couch. It's the terror of watching your partner pack their bags, taking the Netflix password with them. So, you throw out a rushed, half-assed apology, hoping it'll keep them from running out the door. Spoiler alert: it doesn't work long-term.

Next on our tour of terror, we have the fear of being alone. Ah yes, the classic existential dread of solitude. You'd rather apologize for crimes you didn't commit than face the horror of eating dinner by yourself. Fear-based apologies here are like putting a band-aid on a gaping wound; it's a feeble attempt to avoid the dark abyss of loneliness. You say sorry because the thought of scrolling through dating apps again makes you want to cry.

And then there's the fear of being abandoned. This one's a real kicker. It's the fear that your partner will realize you're not as perfect as you pretend to be and leave you for someone who isn't a total screw-up. So, you apologize out of sheer panic, hoping they'll overlook your flaws and stick around. It's like trying to hide a forest fire with a fog machine—utterly pointless but desperate.

Fear-based apologies are nothing more than a quick fix, a way to stave off disaster for a little longer. They're like using a paper towel to clean up a flood—ineffective and kinda pathetic. But hey, we've all been there, right? It's human nature to cling to the familiar, even if it's held together by the flimsiest of threads.

In the next sections, we'll dive deeper into these fears, dissecting each one like a frog in a high school biology class. Get ready to squirm.

### Fear of the Relationship Ending

Alright, let's zoom in on one of the biggest fears driving those flimsy apologies: the fear of the relationship ending. This is the granddaddy of all fears, the one that turns rational adults into groveling messes. You know what I'm talking about—the moment when you realize you've messed up so badly that your partner might actually leave you. Cue the cold sweat and desperate, barely coherent apologies.

Picture this: You're standing there, staring at your partner, who looks like they're about two seconds away from packing up and heading out. Your mind races through all the terrifying possibilities: eating takeout alone, explaining to your mom why you're single again, and the horror of updating your relationship status on social media. To avoid this nightmare, you blurt out the stock apology you've been regurgitating since preschool.

But let's be honest here—these fear-fueled apologies are about as convincing as a toddler promising they won't eat the cookie you just put in front of them.

They're shallow, desperate, and driven by pure panic. You're not really sorry; you're just terrified of facing the consequences.

Take the case of my clients, Brian and Lisa. Brian's idea of romance was leaving the toilet seat up and forgetting anniversaries. One day, Lisa had enough. She packed a bag and was halfway out the door when Brian, in a fit of sheer terror, started apologizing like his life depended on it. And in a way, it did—at least the part of his life that involved not eating microwaved dinners alone.

Brian's apologies were a mess of clichés and empty promises: "I'll change, I swear!" and "I can't live without you!" Classic fear-based drivel. He wasn't thinking about how to actually make things right; he was just trying to stop Lisa from leaving. Spoiler: it didn't work. Lisa saw right through his panicked pleas and left anyway, because even she knew a sinking ship when she saw one.

Fear of the relationship ending makes us act like cornered animals, desperate to save ourselves rather than genuinely fix the problem. It's not about understanding or empathy; it's about self-preservation. And while it might buy you a little time, it won't fix what's fundamentally broken. So next time you feel that icy grip of fear, take a breath and think about what you're really apologizing for. Because fear might keep you afloat for a while, but it's love that will keep you sailing smoothly in the long run.

## Fear of Being Alone

Now, let's tackle another delightful motivator for those hollow apologies: the fear of being alone. The fear of being alone is about dreading Netflix marathons with just your cat, while the fear of the relationship ending is the panic of losing your favorite cuddle buddy and their precious half of the bed. Both fears make you say sorry, but for wildly different and equally ridiculous reasons. The fear of being alone is a real gem. You'd think we're all mature adults who can handle a little solitude, but nope. The moment we get a whiff of potential singlehood, we turn into groveling, pathetic versions of ourselves, desperate to avoid eating takeout for one.

Imagine this scenario: You've been a royal pain in the ass, and your partner has finally had enough. Suddenly, the prospect of Netflix marathons without a cuddle buddy becomes all too real. Panic sets in. You start apologizing, not because you've had an epiphany about your behavior, but because the thought of sitting alone in a restaurant makes you break out in hives. It's like being on the Titanic and deciding that maybe an apology can double as a lifeboat.

Take Jane and Mike, for example. Jane was always nitpicking and criticizing Mike for the tiniest things. One day, Mike decided he'd had enough and started packing his bags. Cue Jane's immediate descent into apology mode. She wasn't sorry for being a nag; she was sorry she might have to spend Saturday nights alone with her cat. Her apologies came out like a bad karaoke performance—off-key and desperate.

Jane's fear of being alone was so palpable, you could almost see the loneliness monster lurking behind her, ready to pounce. Her apologies were just a frantic attempt to keep Mike from walking out the door and leaving her to face the silence of an empty apartment. She didn't care about fixing the underlying issues; she just wanted to avoid the crushing solitude.

Fear of being alone is a powerful driver. It makes us say and do things we don't mean, all in the name of avoiding our own company. We throw out apologies like confetti, hoping that one of them will stick and convince our partner to stay. But these apologies are as hollow as a chocolate Easter bunny. They might look good on the outside, but there's nothing substantial inside.

## Fear of Abandonment

Next up in our parade of sad motivations is the fear of abandonment. This one's the pièce de résistance of fear-based apologies. It's not just about being alone; it's the gut-wrenching dread that someone might actually reject you and leave you behind, exposing you as the flawed human being you are.

Picture Alex and Chris. Alex has deep-seated abandonment issues stemming from a childhood where his parents treated "family time" like a monthly obligation. Anytime Chris so much as hinted at dissatisfaction, Alex would spiral into a panic. His apologies came faster than a bad first date's exit strategy. But let's be real—Alex wasn't apologizing because he genuinely wanted to make things right. No, he was apologizing because the thought of Chris leaving triggered his abandonment alarm louder than a fire drill.

Alex's apologies were a desperate attempt to keep Chris from discovering that he might be better off without him. "I'm sorry, I'm sorry, I'm sorry!" became his mantra, not because he was actually reflecting on his actions, but because he was terrified of being left in the dust. He'd say whatever he thought Chris wanted to hear, as long as it meant Chris would stay.

These kinds of apologies are like using a sponge to stop a dam from breaking—utterly futile and more about stemming the immediate flood of fear than addressing the actual problem. They come from a place of desperation, not genuine remorse or a desire to improve.

Fear of abandonment turns people into puppets, yanking their strings to make them dance the "sorry" dance. But these apologies are more about self-preservation than relationship preservation. They're about keeping the other person around to fill that gaping hole inside, not about making amends or growing together.

In the grand scheme of things, fear-based apologies might buy you a little time. They might keep your partner from walking out the door for now, but they won't stop them from eventually realizing that the foundation of your relationship is about as stable as a house of cards in a hurricane.

## Cultural Perspectives on Fear-based Apologies

Now, let's broaden our horizons a bit and look at how different cultures handle fear-based apologies. You might think this is a universal human screw-up, but oh no, folks, it gets way more colorful. Fear, pride, and ego—these are the spices that make the apology stew simmer differently around the world.

First, let's hop over to Japan. The Japanese have perfected the art of fear-based apologies. Here, the fear of social shame and dishonor is like a national pastime. They have a term for it: "Tatemae," which means doing what's expected on the outside while hiding true feelings. It's like they're all starring in a never-ending soap opera, where every apology is a desperate attempt to save face and avoid public disgrace. Imagine Kenji, who screws up at work and bows so low during his apology, he practically kisses the floor. He's not sorry because he wants to right a wrong; he's terrified of becoming the office pariah. It's a high-stakes game of saving face, and losing means social suicide.

Next, let's take a stroll through the Middle East, where pride and honor are intertwined like strands of a complex tapestry. As the son of an Israeli and married to a woman with Moroccan family I can attest that pride and honor are dense issues that never cease to surprise me.

Here, fear-based apologies are all about avoiding dishonor to the family. Imagine Ahmed, who made a mistake that could bring shame to his family. His apology isn't just about smoothing things over with his partner; it's about preventing the entire clan from being dragged through the mud. He'll say sorry a thousand times over, not out of genuine remorse, but out of fear that his misstep will tarnish the family name for generations. It's a melodrama where pride and fear tango in a dance of desperation.

In many cultures, fear and pride are the twin engines driving apologies. They're not about healing or growth; they're about avoiding the public flogging of reputation. It's less "I'm sorry" and more "Please don't make me a social outcast." These fear-based apologies are as hollow as a politician's promises, meant to keep the social order intact rather than mend any real emotional wounds.

When you're crafting that next apology, maybe take a page from these cultural playbooks. Not because they're doing it right, but because they're a perfect example of what happens when fear and pride take the wheel. Apologies become performances, and relationships are left with the emotional depth of a kiddie pool.

Also, if you happen to be married to someone who comes from a culture where apologizing is viewed so drastically differently than your own, keep in mind that this may play a part in understanding why there's so much friction between the two of you in this area of your relationship.

In the next parts, we'll shift gears and look at how love can transform these hollow gestures into something genuinely meaningful. But for now, remember this: if your apologies are driven by fear, you're just spinning your wheels in the mud.

## Love-based Apologies

Alright, folks, it's time to put on our big kid pants and talk about something a little more evolved: love-based apologies. If fear-based apologies are the diet soda of the apology world—empty and unsatisfying—then love-based apologies are the fine wine: complex, mature, and infinitely more fulfilling.

When you apologize out of love, you're not just trying to avoid the icy silence of the doghouse. You're genuinely invested in making things right because you care about your partner and the relationship. It's not about dodging the fallout; it's about cleaning up the mess because you know the relationship deserves better. It's the mature, grown-up way to say "I'm sorry," and let's be honest, it's rare enough to be considered an endangered species.

Love-based apologies require a level of self-awareness and humility that's about as common as a unicorn sighting. You have to admit to yourself that you're not perfect, that you've messed up, and that your partner's feelings actually matter. It's like looking in the mirror and acknowledging the zit on your nose instead of pretending it's not there. It's real, it's raw, and it's necessary.

Think about Sarah and Tom. Sarah, in a moment of clarity, realizes she's been taking Tom for granted. Instead of a half-hearted "sorry" while staring at her phone, she sits him down, looks him in the eye, and genuinely apologizes. She doesn't just say the words; she explains why she's sorry, what she's learned, and how she's going to do better. This isn't about avoiding a fight or keeping Tom from leaving; it's about growing and improving together. Sarah's apology is rooted in love, and it shows.

Another key aspect of love-based apologies is empathy. You're not just saying sorry because you should; you're saying it because you've taken the time to understand how your actions affected your partner. It's about stepping into their shoes and feeling the blisters you've caused. Empathy transforms a generic "I'm sorry" into a heartfelt "I'm truly sorry because I understand the pain I've caused you."

And let's not forget the willingness to appear imperfect. Love-based apologies often involve sacrificing your image. You have to be okay with your partner seeing you at your most vulnerable, admitting that you're not the infallible hero you'd like to be. It's about breaking down those walls of ego and showing your partner that you're human, flaws and all.

## Sacrificing Image for the Partner's Sake

It's time to tackle one of the toughest parts of a love-based apology: sacrificing your precious image. Let's be real—no one likes admitting they're wrong. We'd all prefer to strut around like peacocks, showing off our perfect feathers. But in the world of real, grown-up relationships, sometimes you've got to pluck a few feathers and show your bare, imperfect self.

When you apologize out of love, you have to be willing to look like a fool. It's about dropping the act and admitting that you're not the flawless superhero you pretend to be. And guess what? That's okay. In fact, it's necessary. Your partner needs to see that you're human, that you make mistakes, and that you're willing to own up to them.

Take Mia and James, for example. Mia's been strutting around like she's the relationship queen, brushing off James's concerns about her emotional unavailability. She's been more focused on keeping up appearances than actually being present in the relationship. When the reality finally hits her, it's like a slap in the face with a wet fish. Mia realizes that if she wants to keep James, she needs to ditch the perfection act and get real.

So, she sits James down and says, "Look, I've been a jerk. I've been so caught up in my own world that I've ignored your feelings. I'm sorry, and I know I need to change." This isn't just an apology; it's a declaration of war against her own ego. Mia's willing to sacrifice her image to show James that she genuinely cares.

This kind of vulnerability is like kryptonite for relationships—in a good way. It breaks down walls and builds trust. When you show your partner that you're willing to be imperfect, it makes them feel safer to admit their own flaws. It's a win-win.

Now, let's talk about Kyle and Lisa. Kyle's always had a bit of a hero complex. He loves being the guy who has all the answers, the one who never makes mistakes. But when Lisa points out that he's been dismissive and arrogant, Kyle's world starts to crumble. He realizes he's been more focused on looking good than actually being good.

So, Kyle takes a deep breath and says, "Lisa, I've been an arrogant ass. I've been so wrapped up in my own ego that I haven't been listening to you. I'm really sorry, and I want to work on this." It's a tough pill to swallow, but Kyle's willingness to sacrifice his image shows Lisa that he's committed to making things right.

Remember, sacrificing your image doesn't mean you're weak. It means you're strong enough to be honest. It means you value your partner and your relationship more than your own pride. It's about showing that you're in this together, flaws and all.

In the next parts, we'll explore more cultural examples and dive into the practical steps of crafting these heartfelt apologies. But for now, just remember: being willing to look like a fool might be the smartest move you ever make. So, get ready to pluck a few feathers and let your true self shine. Your relationship will be all the better for it.

## Cultural Perspectives on Love-based Apologies

Let's take a grand tour around the globe and see how different cultures handle love-based apologies. Spoiler alert: some do it better than others, but all of them have something to teach us about humility, empathy, and sacrificing our precious egos.

First stop: Scandinavia. Picture this—Vikings with their big, burly beards and intimidating axes. You'd think their apologies would be as rough and tough as they are, right? Wrong. Scandinavians have mastered the art of humility in a way that would make a monk blush. In these icy lands, honesty and directness are the name of the game.

When Sven realizes he's been a total blockhead to Ingrid, he doesn't mumble some half-hearted sorry. No, he looks her in the eye, owns up to his mistakes, and promises to do better. It's simple, it's sincere, and it's effective. Plus, the whole "honor and integrity" thing really helps smooth things over. Scandinavian countries spend quite a lot of time focusing on emotional intelligence in their culture and in their schools - I think that has a lot to do with why this is so common.

Next, let's head south to sunny South Africa, where the concept of Ubuntu reigns supreme. Ubuntu is all about community, togetherness, and the idea that "I am because we are." It's like a warm, fuzzy blanket of interconnectedness. When a wife screws up and hurts her husband, she doesn't just apologize for her actions. She acknowledges the ripple effect it has on their community. The wife's apology is steeped in empathy and a genuine desire to restore harmony. She's not just saying sorry to her husband; she's saying sorry to everyone affected by her actions. It's a group hug of an apology, and it's beautiful.

Finally, let's jet over to South Korea, where apologies are a bit like a dramatic scene from a K-drama. There's a lot of bowing, a lot of heartfelt words, and maybe even some tears if you're lucky. In South Korea, relationships are deeply valued, and apologies are a way to show that you're willing to put the other person's feelings above your own pride. When Min-Jae messes up with Soo-Jin, he's not afraid to get a little emotional. He bows deeply, expresses his sincere regret, and promises to be better. It's not just about saving face; it's about showing that he's truly committed to making amends.

So, what do these cultural lessons teach us? Whether it's the straightforward honesty of the Scandinavians, the communal empathy of the South Africans, or the emotional sincerity of the South Koreans, love-based apologies are all about putting the relationship first. It's about being willing to look a little silly, to admit you're wrong, and to show your partner that you genuinely care about their feelings.

Incorporating these cultural nuggets into your own apologies can take them from mediocre to magnificent. So next time you're in the doghouse, channel your inner Viking, embrace the spirit of Ubuntu, or add a touch of K-drama flair. Your partner will appreciate the effort, and your relationship will be all the stronger for it.

# Apology Hall of Shame:
# Juul's Teen Vaping Crisis 2019

Ah, Juul. If there was ever a masterclass in how not to apologize, Juul's 2019 teen vaping fiasco takes the cake. By now, we all know that apologies driven by fear are about as useful as a cup of coffee is to an insomniac. Yet, Juul's attempt to say "sorry" was as authentic as a three-dollar bill.

### The Incident

In 2019, Juul got caught with its hand in the cookie jar. Their marketing tactics, flashy ads with young, vibrant models, were practically screaming, "Hey kids, come and get it!" Surprise, surprise, teens flocked to their products like seagulls to a beach picnic. Parents were furious, health experts were alarmed, and lawmakers were ready to pounce. Juul was in deep trouble and needed to clean up its act fast.

### The Failed Apology

Enter Juul's CEO at the time, Kevin Burns, who offered up this gem of an apology:

*"We never intended for our product to be used by underage individuals. We are committed to preventing underage use, and we have taken significant steps to address this issue."*

Riveting, isn't it? This apology could put an insomniac to sleep. It was clear Juul was more afraid of legal repercussions than genuinely sorry. Where did it go wrong? Let's break it down.

First off, the apology was as insincere as a reality TV romance. It read like a carefully crafted PR statement, not a heartfelt admission of guilt. And vague? "Significant steps to address this issue" is about as clear as mud. What steps? Who knows! They certainly didn't spell them out. To top it off, the line "never intended" subtly shifted blame, as if teens just stumbled upon Juul's products by sheer accident.

Naturally, the public didn't buy it. Social media exploded with criticism, parents were enraged, and lawmakers sharpened their pitchforks. Memes mocking the apology flooded the internet, and Juul became the poster child for corporate irresponsibility. Regulatory bodies weren't impressed either, leading to numerous investigations and legal challenges.

## The Better Apology

So, how should Juul have handled this? Here's what a better apology, one that doesn't make you roll your eyes, might have looked like:

*We deeply regret and take full responsibility for our marketing practices that have contributed to the rise in teen vaping. Our actions were misguided, and we apologize to the parents, teens, and communities affected. Effective immediately, we are halting all advertising and implementing stricter age verification processes. We are committing millions of dollars to fund educational programs aimed at preventing teen vaping and to support addiction recovery services. We understand that words alone are not enough, and we pledge to earn back your trust through our actions.*

This apology works because it sounds like they actually care. While a corporation can't show "love" effectively for its consumers or the public at large, care and compassion for doing what benefits society is the corporate equivalent of love.

Additionally, this apology admits fault, outlines specific actions they're taking to fix the problem, and even puts some money where their mouth is. By apologizing out of genuine concern for their customers, Juul could have started to rebuild trust instead of landing themselves in the Apology Hall of Shame.

# 14

# Blame Hollywood: How Media Messes with Apologies

ALRIGHT, LET'S FACE IT: the American education system does a bang-up job of cramming quadratic equations and the periodic table down our throats, but when it comes to teaching Emotional Quotient (EQ) and social interaction? Nada. Zilch. They seem to think we'll just magically figure out how to be emotionally intelligent, like sprouting a third arm overnight. We don't.

But hey, it's not just the schools. The American public has another punching bag for our collective emotional illiteracy: the media.

The media is a masterclass in how to mess up emotional literacy. TV shows and movies serve up apologies that are as authentic as a Kardashian's Instagram post. Reality shows? Don't even get me started. These train wrecks are emotional junk food, masquerading as real-life drama, teaching us all the wrong lessons about conflict resolution and forgiveness. News programs are no better, sensationalizing apologies for ratings, reducing genuine human emotion to clickbait fodder.

Add social media to this toxic cocktail and you have a perfect storm of emotional dysfunction. People think a hashtag can substitute for a heartfelt apology. It can't. And don't get me started on social justice movements hijacking the apology narrative for their own agendas. Suddenly, saying sorry is a political act, not a personal one.

So, yes, it's an uphill battle. Between Hollywood, cable news, and the dumpster fire that is social media, it's a miracle any of us know how to say sorry and mean it. This is the battleground we're up against, folks. And let's be honest, the odds are not in our favor.

In this chapter I'm going to be going over several examples from some TV shows, Movies and other media moments. I know how triggered people can get by revealing plot points and twists in movies and shows they haven't seen so if you're one of those with thin skin who gets annoyed when a show that's been off the air for years is "spoiled" by reading about it, consider yourself warned.

## When Media Tries to Get It Right: Pride in Breaking Bad

Sometimes, the media stumbles upon the truth and actually portrays pride as the destructive force it is. Case in point: Walter White from *Breaking Bad*. This guy went from a downtrodden high school chemistry teacher to a meth kingpin, all because of one deadly sin—pride. He wasn't just cooking meth to make ends meet; he wanted to be the best, the Heisenberg of the meth world.

Let's talk about the scene where his pride really sealed his fate. Picture this: Season 5, Episode 14, "Ozymandias." Walter's world is crumbling around him. He's lost his family, his empire, and his health is failing. Yet, in the midst of this chaos, his ego is still calling the shots. Hank, his brother-in-law and DEA agent, is on his knees, at the mercy of Jack's gang. Walter, desperate to save Hank, pleads with Jack, offering his entire $80 million fortune. But Hank, showing more dignity in his final moments than Walter ever did, looks at him and says, "You're the smartest guy I ever met, and you're too stupid to see. He made up his mind ten minutes ago." Jack shoots Hank, and Walter's pride is left with blood on its hands.

Walter's pride didn't just push him into the meth business; it drove him to build an empire, to be recognized, to be feared. It was never just about providing for his family. It was about being the best, about showing everyone that Walter White was someone to be reckoned with. And that pride? It was his ultimate downfall. He lost his family, his freedom, and in the end, his life.

Yet, here's the kicker: despite all this, people loved Walter White. They admired his ingenuity, his intellect, his sheer determination. He was the antihero we couldn't help but root for, even as he spiraled deeper into his own hubris. Sure, the show tried to paint him as the villain who let his ego get in the way of everything good in his life. But the sad truth is, Walter's likability undermined that message.

Even when Hollywood tries to get it right, it often fails because we, the audience, are suckers for a complex character. We see ourselves in their flaws, their struggles, and we empathize with them. The more sophisticated the storytelling, the more we connect with these flawed characters, and the more we might find ourselves emulating those same destructive behaviors in real life. Walter White's pride was supposed to be a cautionary tale, but for many, it was a blueprint for justifying their own ego-driven decisions.

## The Social Network:
## Pride, Apologies, and the Downfall That Wasn't

For another example, let's turn to the 2010 movie *The Social Network*. This gem of a film offers a triple threat: a true story, social media, and the tragic tale of how pride and ego can wreck relationships. It's a masterclass in how not to apologize, brought to you by the king of emotional incompetence himself, Mark Zuckerberg. Remember how we talked about his botched apology during the Cambridge Analytica scandal? Yeah, same guy.

The plot of *The Social Network* follows Zuckerberg's meteoric rise from a socially awkward Harvard student to the billionaire founder of Facebook. It's a tale of ambition, betrayal, and a complete inability to take accountability. Throughout the movie, Zuckerberg bulldozes through friendships, partnerships, and potential romantic interests without a single genuine apology. His hubris is on full display, wrapped up in a hoodie and flip-flops.

One scene, in particular, captures the essence of his pride and insecurity. Near the climax of the film, we find Zuckerberg being sued by his former friend and business partner, Eduardo Saverin. As Eduardo confronts him in a heated meeting, the tension is palpable. Eduardo, in a fit of rage, slams his laptop on the table, shattering the illusion of their friendship. "You better lawyer up, asshole, because I'm not coming back for 30%. I'm coming back for everything," Eduardo seethes. Meanwhile, Zuckerberg sits there, expressionless, unable to muster a shred of accountability or remorse. His silence speaks volumes, his pride refusing to let him admit any fault.

This scene is a vivid illustration of how Zuckerberg's inability to apologize or take accountability cost him dearly. His refusal to acknowledge Eduardo's contributions and feelings led to the dissolution of a pivotal relationship in his life. Pride, once again, proves to be the fatal flaw. The film tries to portray this moment as a critical juncture, a cautionary tale of ego leading to personal ruin. But does it really?

In the final scene, Zuckerberg is seen alone in a conference room, refreshing the Facebook page, waiting to see if a girl he likes has accepted his friend request. It's a pitiful image, highlighting his inability to make genuine human connections. Rather than picking up the phone and having an honest conversation, he hides behind a screen, waiting for validation in the form of a digital thumbs-up. This scene underscores his failure to confront his own shortcomings and seek real human interaction.

Despite Hollywood's best efforts to frame these shortcomings as the downfall of an empire, let's look at the reality. Who is Mark Zuckerberg? The founder of Facebook, a billionaire, a man whose company influences elections and shapes global conversations. Did Facebook crumble? No. Did its stock plummet? Nope. It remains one of the most formidable companies on the planet. And did Mark Zuckerberg end up alone in a puddle of his own misery? Absolutely not. He got married, has a family, and from all public appearances, leads a happy life.

So, what's the real cost here? A few awkward moments where he couldn't ask a girl out? That's not exactly a tragedy. It sends the message that if you want to get ahead, avoid apologies, suffer minor discomfort, and you'll still come out on top. The people you hurt? They're just collateral damage. Great job, Hollywood. Stellar lesson for our kids.

Now, let's not kid ourselves. It's not Hollywood's job to be the moral compass for society. But with its massive influence, it has an undeniable impact on public behavior. If we can't critique these narratives and their negative effects, we lose our ability to debate and think critically about these issues. So yes, it's time to call out these toxic portrayals and strive for better, more nuanced storytelling that doesn't glamorize emotional incompetence.

## Kevin Hart's Oscars Controversy: When Pride and Apologies Collide

Let's dive into the Kevin Hart's Oscars controversy in 2019. This debacle is a perfect case study in how pride can turn a simple "I'm sorry" into a public fiasco. So, Kevin Hart gets tapped to host the 2019 Oscars. Big deal, right? Until the internet dredges up some of his old homophobic tweets. Instead of doing the sensible thing and issuing a quick apology, Hart decides to dig his heels in. "I've addressed this before," he basically says, with all the humility of a Kardashian on a red carpet. His pride was front and center, refusing to bow to what he saw as unjustified outrage. And what happens when you throw pride into the mix? The flames just get higher. Kevin, buddy, you could have doused this fire with a few sincere words, but no, you had to let pride turn it into a full-blown inferno.

## Forced Apology Under Public Pressure

As the backlash grew, so did the pressure. Eventually, Hart caved and issued an apology. But let's be real, it felt as sincere as a reality star's wedding vows. He only apologized after stepping down from hosting the Oscars, making it clear the apology wasn't from the heart but from the PR team. This whole fiasco shows how public pressure can force out an apology that's about as genuine as a spray tan. The media circus turned this personal issue into public theater, showing us all how pride can complicate what should be a straightforward act of contrition.

## The Impact on Public Perception

Hart's proud refusal and subsequent forced apology split public opinion right down the middle. Some fans praised his initial defiance, while others saw him as a coward ducking responsibility. The division was almost as entertaining as the actual controversy. Pride didn't just affect Hart; it polarized the entire audience, making genuine forgiveness harder to come by. The media, of course, had a field day, amplifying the drama to a deafening roar. Who knew a comedian's old tweets could turn into such a spectacle?

## The Tragedy of Diluting Comedy

Here's where it gets truly tragic. Comedy is one of the few bastions of our society that thrives on controversy and edge. Comedians push the envelope, and that's what makes them funny. Demand apologies from them every time they tow the line of appropriateness, and you kill the essence of comedy itself. The biggest tragedy of the Kevin Hart scenario is that he initially chose the right path: he stood by his comment as a joke. But the relentless pressure from his PR team and the public forced him into an insincere apology, which only serves to dilute the power of apologies as a whole. And to top it off, he didn't even get to host the Oscars. So we all lost.

We lost the opportunity to see someone at their prime make the Oscars ceremony fun. We lost a sense of freedom in comedy, which is crucial to its success. And Kevin Hart lost his moral compass, caving to a mob looking for a scapegoat to thrust their agenda onto. This fiasco underscores the precarious balance comedians must navigate between pushing boundaries and facing the wrath of a hypersensitive audience.

## Lessons in Humility and Accountability

Here's the kicker: this whole mess could have been a masterclass in humility and accountability. Instead, it was a cautionary tale of how not to handle an apology. Hart's reluctance to immediately own up and his eventual, painfully insincere apology serve as a stark reminder: genuine apologies require you to swallow your pride and take full responsibility. Pride delayed this process, leading to greater fallout and prolonged public scrutiny. Kevin, if you're reading this, take notes for next time. Either stand by your joke and don't apologize ever ever ever for trying to be funny (that would be my preference), or apologize right away. Don't split the difference. You lose out on both sides.

## Media's Role in Shaping Apology Narratives

And let's not forget the media's role in this circus. By constantly spotlighting Hart's tweets and his responses, the media turned up the heat, influencing public perception and intensifying the backlash. It's a perfect example of how media coverage can escalate a situation, making it harder for genuine remorse to cut through the noise. The media reflects and shapes societal expectations around apologies and accountability, and in Hart's case, they turned a personal misstep into a national debate.

Kevin Hart's Oscars controversy is a textbook example of how pride can derail the apology process. It shows how public pressure can force insincere apologies and highlights the media's role in complicating personal accountability.

## Cancel Culture: Good Intentions, Bad Execution

Cancel culture is the social media version of a medieval witch hunt. These days, people are pressured to apologize for the smallest things—stuff that wasn't even an issue until some loud minority of social justice warriors decided to dig up skeletons from the past. These weren't just skeletons; they were practically fossils, relics of a different time and context. Yet here we are, scrutinizing them with the intensity of a conspiracy theorist on a caffeine binge.

## The Apology Paradox

Here's the kicker: even when you do apologize, it's never good enough. You could issue the most heartfelt, tear-jerking apology, and guess what? You're still canceled. After all, it's not apology culture, it's cancel culture. It's like a dystopian game where the rules are made up on the fly, and no matter what you do, you lose. This madness takes away any motivation to apologize, turning what should be a healing process into a public flogging. If we stop modeling what a genuine apology can do, we're going to stop trying them in our personal lives. And trust me, that's a world you don't want to live in.

## James Gunn's Firing from Disney

In 2018, James Gunn, the genius behind *Guardians of the Galaxy*, gets canned because someone unearthed decade-old tweets filled with dark humor. Yeah, they were in poor taste, but Gunn had already apologized for them years ago. He'd moved on, grown as a person, and here comes Disney, acting like a puritanical nanny, firing him faster than you can say "hypocrite." The backlash was so intense, it was like watching a Marvel movie, complete with a triumphant return when Disney reinstated him. This wasn't justice; it was a farce.

## Alison Roman's Temporary Fall from Grace

Food writer and chef Alison Roman critiqued Chrissy Teigen's cooking empire and Marie Kondo's product line, and suddenly, she's the culinary antichrist. People screamed "racism" and "elitism" faster than they could say "Instagram-mable avocado toast." The *New York Times* put her column on hold, and the internet mob had a field day. Roman was making a point about commercialization, not launching a personal attack. But in the cancel culture arena, context is as dead as disco. She apologized, sincerely at that, but the damage was done. It was overkill, plain and simple.

## Matt Damon's Misunderstood Comments

In 2017, Matt Damon dared to suggest that not all accusations in the #MeToo movement should be treated equally. He wanted a nuanced conversation—imagine that! But his comments were twisted out of context, making him look like the poster boy for victim-blaming. The internet mob didn't just cancel him; they dragged him through the virtual mud. Damon clarified his stance, supported the movement, but the damage was irreversible. His attempt to provoke thoughtful discussion turned into a public crucifixion.

## J.K. Rowling's Opinion on Trans Issues

And then there's J.K. Rowling, who expressed her views on transgender issues and ended up being labeled as the Dark Lord of transphobia. Her opinions, based on her understanding of biological sex, sparked a wildfire of outrage. People were ready to toss their Harry Potter books into a bonfire. What's ridiculous here is that she was expressing a personal belief, not inciting violence or hate. Canceling someone for their opinion, especially in a nuanced and ongoing debate, is peak absurdity. It's a dangerous precedent where intellectual debate is suffocated, and dissenting voices are silenced.

These instances show how cancel culture misfires, turning what should be opportunities for dialogue and growth into public lynchings. The rush to judgment ignores the complexity of human behavior and the possibility of redemption. It's a sobering reminder that the court of public opinion often gets it horribly wrong.

## Apologies on Social Media: The Digital Trainwrecks

In the age of social media, the art of the apology has been reduced to a few hundred characters, served up on platforms like Instagram and Twitter. These bite-sized apologies often lack sincerity, depth, and any meaningful attempt at making amends. Instead, they come off as half-hearted attempts to placate the masses, ticking a box rather than addressing the core issue. The brevity of these platforms makes it nearly impossible to convey genuine remorse, resulting in a slew of public apologies that are as ineffective as they are cringe-worthy.

Let's face it: social media apologies are often just public relations stunts. They are crafted not to express true contrition but to manage public perception and minimize damage. The following examples showcase how disastrously these digital apologies can backfire, turning a bad situation into a full-blown public relations nightmare.

Take Logan Paul, for instance. In 2018, this YouTuber extraordinaire decided to film a vlog in Japan's Aokigahara forest, also known as the Suicide Forest. His video, which featured the body of a suicide victim, was riddled with insensitive comments and blatant disrespect. The internet rightfully erupted in outrage.

Instead of immediately recognizing his grotesque mistake and taking sincere steps to make amends, Paul dashed off a half-hearted apology on Twitter. He claimed, "I didn't do it for views," and tried to spin the fiasco as a misguided attempt to raise awareness about mental health. The internet wasn't buying it.

His apology felt more like a bad marketing pitch than a genuine expression of remorse. As the backlash intensified, Paul released a follow-up video apology, but the damage was done. The public saw through his attempts to salvage his image, recognizing his apology as insincere and self-serving.

Then there's Paula Deen, the celebrity chef who found herself in hot water over accusations of using racial slurs and harboring a history of racist behavior. When the allegations surfaced, Deen's response was a masterclass in how not to apologize.

She released a choppy, poorly edited video on YouTube that seemed hastily thrown together. If her goal was to appear regretful, she failed spectacularly. The video felt disjointed and lacked any semblance of genuine remorse.

Recognizing the backlash, she issued a second, equally awkward apology video. Rather than mending her public image, these attempts only served to further alienate her audience. The rushed, amateurish nature of her apologies made them come off as insincere, highlighting the critical flaw in using social media to address deep-seated issues.

Kevin Spacey's Twitter apology is another prime example of a celebrity mismanaging a crisis. Amid the #MeToo movement, multiple allegations of sexual misconduct surfaced against Spacey.

Instead of issuing a straightforward apology, Spacey used the opportunity to come out as gay. His tweet was a jarring mix of addressing the accusations and announcing his sexual orientation, a move seen as a blatant deflection.

By conflating his coming out with serious allegations of assault, Spacey managed to offend both the LGBTQ+ community and the victims of his alleged misconduct. The apology was perceived as manipulative and insincere, doing nothing to quell the outrage but instead exacerbating it. His attempt to pivot the conversation away from the accusations backfired, cementing his fall from grace and it was all on Twitter.

Lena Dunham also managed to botch a public apology on Twitter. When her friend Murray Miller was accused of sexual assault, Dunham publicly defended him, claiming the accusation was one of the few false reports. This statement sparked immediate backlash, given her vocal advocacy for believing victims.

Her subsequent apology on Twitter expressed regret for her comments, but it reeked of damage control rather than genuine remorse. The hypocrisy in her initial defense and subsequent apology was glaring.

Dunham's actions and words were at odds, leading many to question her integrity and commitment to supporting survivors. Her apology, intended to mend the rift, instead highlighted her inconsistency and further damaged her credibility.

These examples illustrate the inherent flaws in using social media for apologies. The brevity and performative nature of these platforms often strip away the sincerity and depth required for a genuine apology. Social media influencers and celebrities need to understand that issuing an apology on these platforms is not a substitute for real, meaningful contrition. An effective apology should go beyond a few hastily typed characters; it should include a video clip showing genuine remorse, an attempt at restitution, or an interview that allows for clarity and engagement with the affected community without the need to feel rushed or boxed into a character limit.

Moreover, these influencers are inadvertently training their followers to believe that a social media apology is sufficient to mend any rift. This is far from the truth. An apology is about repairing a relationship, not just clearing oneself of accountability in front of a digital jury. When apologies become mere public performances, they lose their power to heal and transform. We must strive for apologies that foster genuine understanding and reconciliation, both online and offline.

## Real-World Influence: The Lance Armstrong Debacle

Let's talk about the granddaddy of all public apology fiascos: Lance Armstrong. This guy was the poster child for athletic excellence, winning seven Tour de France titles. Then, it all came crashing down when his doping scandal was exposed. For years, Armstrong had vehemently denied any wrongdoing, attacking and suing anyone who dared to suggest he was anything less than squeaky clean. When the truth finally came out, it was like finding out Santa Claus was actually a con artist running a Ponzi scheme.

Armstrong's apology tour culminated in an interview with Oprah Winfrey. Yes, Oprah. Because when you're trying to claw your way back into the public's good graces, who better to confess your sins to than the queen of daytime TV? The whole setup was so over-the-top, it felt like Armstrong was trying to win an Oscar for Best Performance in a Faux Apology. Sitting across from Oprah, he finally admitted to doping, but it came off as a well-rehearsed PR stunt rather than a moment of genuine remorse.

The result? Armstrong never really regained his popularity. People saw through the charade. His attempt at an apology was seen as too little, too late. The public wasn't buying what he was selling, and his credibility was left in tatters. This whole spectacle didn't just tarnish Armstrong's reputation; it also managed to warp our collective understanding of what a real apology should look like.

The media's focus on the spectacle rather than the substance sent a clear message: public apologies are more about damage control than genuine contrition. This debacle likely made people more skeptical about apologies in their own lives. After all, if Lance Armstrong can put on an elaborate show and still come off as insincere, what hope do the rest of us have? It reinforced the idea that apologies are just another strategic maneuver to get out of trouble, rather than a heartfelt effort to make things right.

So, thanks, Lance, for turning the public apology into a theatrical farce. Great job on teaching everyone that when it comes to saying sorry, it's all about the performance, not the actual remorse. Now, whenever someone messes up, they can just whip out their acting chops instead of genuinely trying to mend their ways. Bravo.

## The Rise of "Sorry Not Sorry"

Remember the good old days when people actually apologized? Yeah, those days are long gone. Now, apologies are like rotary phones – relics of a bygone era. Enter the era of "sorry not sorry," the catchphrase that took faux regret and unapologetic defiance to new heights. To write an entire chapter on the influence of media and not include a section on the "sorry not sorry" phenomenon you would have to be swimming in the shallow end of the gene pool. This phrase perfectly captures our society's love affair with being dismissive and defiant, all wrapped up in the brevity and sarcasm of the digital age.

## Origins and Peak

The phrase "sorry not sorry" is believed to have originated in the early 2000s, gaining traction on social media platforms like Twitter and Instagram. It quickly became the darling of the younger generation, who used it to express a nonchalant attitude towards actions or opinions they weren't genuinely remorseful about. It was a convenient way to nod to societal expectations of an apology while simultaneously giving the middle finger to the need for actual contrition.

By the mid-2010s, "sorry not sorry" had reached its cultural peak. In 2015, Demi Lovato dropped a song titled "Sorry Not Sorry," which became an anthem for faux apologies everywhere. Lovato's unapologetic delivery turned the phrase into a rallying cry for self-empowerment and defiance against critics. Suddenly, everyone and their grandma were throwing "sorry not sorry" into conversations, memes, and social media captions.

## Cultural Ingraining

The phrase's simplicity and catchiness made it an easy staple in everyday language. It became a meme, a social media caption, and even a marketing slogan. Brands jumped on the bandwagon, using "sorry not sorry" to appeal to the rebellious, younger demographic, conveying boldness and confidence.

Celebrities loved it too. It became their go-to line for brushing off controversies or criticism, allowing them to maintain their public image without appearing weak or overly apologetic. The phrase normalized a dismissive attitude, making it the perfect cop-out for anyone looking to dodge genuine accountability.

## Criticism and Backlash

But let's not kid ourselves – "sorry not sorry" hasn't exactly been embraced by everyone. Critics argue that it undermines the sincerity of apologies and fosters a culture of insensitivity and irresponsibility and I proudly count myself as one of those critics. It's like the perfect tool for promoting a dismissive attitude toward remorse, discouraging genuine accountability and reflection.

I've seen the fallout of this phrase in dozens of my counseling sessions. Couples come in, and the moment one of them pulls out the "sorry not sorry" card, it's like tossing a grenade into the room. Trust me, it never does anything but piss off their partner (and me, for that matter). When you're trying to rebuild intimacy and your partner says, "I'm not sorry for having needs you can't meet," you're basically hitting a dead end.

I'll never forget the moment I realized how far this had infiltrated our culture. A couple was arguing about how bad the wife was at apologizing. In a fit of exasperation, she said, "I just don't like apologizing, sorry not sorry." The sheer lack of self-awareness actually made my jaw drop involuntarily. It was a pinnacle moment of realizing that this "sorry not sorry" nonsense had gone too far.

The rise of "sorry not sorry" reflects a broader cultural shift towards a more defiant, less remorseful attitude in public and personal interactions. While it can serve as a powerful expression of self-confidence and resistance to undue criticism, it also risks trivializing the importance of genuine apologies and accountability. As the phrase continues to be used and critiqued, it highlights the ongoing tension between maintaining personal integrity and navigating social expectations in the digital age.

## The Apology Circus - Enter at Your Own Risk

So, what have we learned? That the media, in all its glory, has turned the art of apologizing into a sideshow act. Between Hollywood's tragic anti-heroes, social media's bite-sized contrition, and the grand debacles of public figures like Kevin Hart and Lance Armstrong, it's clear that genuine apologies are as rare as a unicorn at a dog show. Instead of fostering real accountability, we've created a circus where the only thing more inflated than the egos are the insincere apologies.

But let's not forget the star of this freak show: cancel culture. This lovely social media phenomenon has ensured that no matter how heartfelt or groveling your apology, it's never quite enough. It's like being stuck in a dystopian game show where the rules change faster than a hacker's IP address, and no matter how many times you spin the wheel, you always land on "canceled." This not only ruins lives but also teaches us that maybe it's better to just skip the apology altogether. Why bother when you're doomed if you do and doomed if you don't?

In the end, it's a sad state of affairs when a sincere "I'm sorry" has become as believable as a reality show plotline. The media's role in shaping this narrative is undeniable, but so is our complicity in eating it up. Maybe it's time to step off this merry-go-round of public contrition and start valuing real, meaningful apologies. Because if we continue down this path, we'll end up in a world where saying sorry is just another performance – and we're all left holding the popcorn, waiting for the next act.

# 15

# Closing Time: Last Call for Apology Wisdom

WELL, HERE WE ARE at the end of our journey together. You've waded through the sea of terrible apologies, navigated the minefield of relationship blunders, and hopefully picked up a thing or two about how to not be a complete disaster when saying sorry. Let's talk about what makes a genuine apology so powerful. It's not just a matter of saying "sorry" and praying the storm blows over. No, a genuine apology is like finding a hidden superpower that can transform your relationship. It's that moment in the movie when the hero finally gets their act together and saves the day. A real apology is more than a word—it's a declaration: "I care enough to fix this mess." When you apologize sincerely, you're not just patching things up—you're building a stronger, more resilient relationship. So, slap on your superhero cape and get ready to work some magic.

Most people approach apologies like they're checking off a grocery list. "Apologize to wife – check. Avoid sleeping on the couch tonight – check." This isn't a chore; it's your relationship on the line! A genuine apology means digging deep, acknowledging the hurt you've caused, and showing you're willing to make amends. It's about saying, "I messed up, and I'm going to do better."

Think of it like this: a real apology is the duct tape that holds your relationship together, even when it feels like it's about to fall apart. There's no substitute for that kind of repair job.

Let's talk about the aftershocks of a genuine apology. You might think saying sorry is the end of the ordeal, but it's just the beginning. A sincere apology sets off a chain reaction of healing and trust-building. When you own up to your mistakes, you're showing your partner that you respect them and value the relationship enough to put in the effort. This isn't about groveling or playing the martyr; it's about being an adult and taking responsibility. And guess what? When your partner sees that you're genuinely sorry, they're more likely to forgive, forget, and maybe even laugh about it later. So, next time you screw up, don't half-ass your apology. Go all in, and watch as your relationship gets stronger than ever.

## Sorry Never Sleeps: The Apology That Keeps On Giving

It's crucial to remember that apologizing isn't a one-and-done deal. Think of it as an ongoing journey, not a destination. You don't just say "sorry" once and expect everything to be perfect forever. Nope, relationships require regular maintenance, much like a car. If you neglect it, eventually it's going to break down, and you'll find yourself stranded on the highway of love with no idea how to fix it. Apologizing is part of that maintenance routine. It's like changing the oil or rotating the tires—essential to keeping things running smoothly.

In this continuous journey, you'll face new challenges and make fresh mistakes. That's just life. The key is to approach each situation with the understanding that apologizing is a skill you'll keep refining. Think of it like learning a new language. At first, you're going to sound like a bumbling idiot, but with practice, you start to get the hang of it. The more you apologize, the better you'll get at it. And just like any skill, it gets easier with time. So, don't beat yourself up if you stumble along the way. Each apology is an opportunity to improve and show your partner that you're committed to growing together.

Let's be clear: this isn't about becoming a doormat who apologizes for everything, including the weather. It's about recognizing when you've screwed up and taking responsibility. It's about making amends and showing your partner that you're willing to put in the effort to keep the relationship healthy. A continuous journey means you're in it for the long haul, ready to navigate the ups and downs together. So, buckle up and embrace the ride. Apologizing is a lifelong skill, and mastering it will not only save your relationship but also enrich your life.

## Mind Reading 101: Mastering the Art of Empathy

Don't forget about empathy and understanding - they are the secret ingredients that turn a mediocre apology into a masterpiece. Empathy isn't just about feeling sorry for someone; it's about stepping into their shoes and really getting why they're upset. It's the difference between saying, "I'm sorry you feel that way," and "I'm sorry I hurt you. I understand why you're upset, and it's my fault." One is a cop-out; the other is a heartfelt acknowledgment of their pain.

Understanding is the partner-in-crime to empathy. It's not enough to just feel bad; you've got to understand what your partner is going through. Imagine you're in a high-stakes game of charades, and your partner is desperately trying to convey how hurt they are. You can't just nod and smile—you've got to figure out what they're really feeling and why. That means listening, really listening, without planning your next rebuttal. It means putting aside your ego and focusing on their experience. When you understand where they're coming from, your apology becomes more than just words—it becomes a bridge to healing.

When you combine empathy and understanding, you're not just saying, "I'm sorry." You're saying, "I'm here with you. I get it, and I'm willing to change." This is what makes an apology stick. It shows your partner that you're not just trying to get out of the doghouse; you're genuinely committed to making things right. So, next time you're in the hot seat, don't just apologize. Dig deep, empathize, and understand. Your relationship will be all the stronger for it, and you'll find that conflicts become opportunities for growth rather than just obstacles to overcome.

### Tips for Winning the Sorry Game

Let's recap some of the key points we've covered to help you master the art of apologizing. First, remember the importance of timing. As we discussed earlier, apologizing in the heat of the moment can often backfire. Give it a bit of time to let emotions settle, but don't let it linger too long. Strike when the iron is warm, not scalding hot or ice cold. This balance is crucial to ensure that your apology is received with the openness it deserves.

Next, tone and body language are critical. We've seen how a genuine apology can be derailed by a sarcastic tone or dismissive body language. Make sure your tone is calm, clear, and sincere. Avoid crossing your arms, rolling your eyes, or any other gestures that might suggest insincerity. Remember, your body speaks as loudly as your words, so make sure it's saying the right thing. As we covered, an apology isn't just about the words you use but how you present them.

Specificity is another crucial aspect we've delved into. A vague apology like, "I'm sorry for whatever I did," doesn't cut it. Be specific about what you did wrong and acknowledge the impact of your actions. For example, "I'm sorry I forgot our anniversary dinner and made you feel unimportant" shows that you've thought about your actions and understand their impact. Following it up with a plan to make amends, like setting reminders or being more mindful, demonstrates a commitment to change. This ties back to the idea that an apology is a promise to do better, not just a quick fix for a mistake.

By keeping these key points in mind - timing, tone, body language, and specificity - you're well on your way to delivering apologies that truly matter. These aren't just tips; they're the building blocks of genuine, heartfelt apologies that can heal and strengthen your relationships.

**Level Up: Transforming Your Apology Game**

Finally, let's talk about what this whole journey of learning to apologize means for your personal growth. Apologizing effectively is more than just fixing a mistake; it's about evolving into a better version of yourself. When you get into the habit of acknowledging your faults and making amends, you're not just doing your relationship a favor—you're becoming a more self-aware and emotionally intelligent person. This is about taking the lessons we've covered and applying them not just in your romantic relationships, but across all areas of your life.

Remember how we discussed the importance of empathy and understanding? Practicing these skills will make you a more compassionate and considerate person. It's not just about saying the right words, but about genuinely understanding and caring for others' feelings. This empathy extends beyond apologies and becomes a core part of who you are. Imagine the impact on your friendships, your work relationships, and even interactions with strangers. You'll find that people respond to you more positively when they see that you genuinely care.

Let's not forget the power of reflection. Throughout this book, we've talked about the importance of looking inward and understanding your own emotional triggers. This self-awareness doesn't just help you apologize better; it helps you navigate life's challenges with more grace and confidence. By continually reflecting on your actions and their impact, you develop a deeper understanding of yourself and the world around you. This kind of personal growth is invaluable. It's the difference between stumbling through life and walking with purpose.

So, take these lessons to heart. Embrace the journey of becoming a better apologizer as part of your broader path to personal growth. You'll find that as you improve your apology skills, you'll also improve your relationships, your self-awareness, and your overall happiness. It's a win-win situation that makes the effort truly worth it.

## Your Mission: Spread the Gospel of Not Sucking at Apologies

Alright, you've made it through the rollercoaster of apology disasters and re-demption. Now, let's talk about what you can do next. First off, do us a solid and write a review on Amazon for this book. Seriously, it helps more than you know. Think of it as your good deed for the day. Your review helps get the word out to people who, like you, are trying to improve their apology game and, by extension, their lives. So, head over to Amazon, type up a few kind words, and let's spread the gospel of not sucking at apologies.

But wait, there's more! If reading this book has made you realize that you might need a little extra help (because, let's face it, some of you do), we've got your back. If you want to work directly with us, you can reach out to us via our website at SuckBooks.com. Our schedules are packed tighter than a clown car, but we prioritize people who have actually read our work. So, drop us a line and let's see if we can squeeze you in.

Don't just sit there basking in the glory of your newfound apology skills. Take action! Write that review and get in touch if you need personalized help. We're here to make sure you don't just learn from this book but actually put it into practice. Remember, an apology without action is like a diet without exercise—useless. So, let's get moving. Write the review, reach out for a session, and start transforming your relationships today. Your future self will thank you, and maybe, just maybe, your apologies will stop being terrible.

# ENJOYING THE BOOK? PLEASE CONSIDER WRITING A REVIEW ON AMAZON

As a small independent publisher, one of the absolute best ways you can support our work is by leaving us a review on Amazon to let people know your honest thoughts about this book.

1. Open the camera on your phone
2. Point the camera at the QR code above
3. Open the link and write an honest review
4. Enjoy our gratitude for your help

Made in the USA
Columbia, SC
03 February 2025

53201417R00124